Get Your Dream Developer Job

How To Find A Job As A New Programmer

CHARLES MAX WOOD

Copyright © 2019 Charles Max Wood. All rights reserved. No part of this book can be reproduced in any form without the written permission of the author and its publisher.

Get a Copy of the Audiobook

Thank you for checking out this manual on finding your dream developer job.

Our process is proven to help you make the most of your programming career and find a place that will help you grow and make you happy.

If you would like a copy of the audio version of this book, then go to the following:

https://devchat.tv/dream-developer-job-audiobook

Table of Contents

Get a Copy of the Audiobook 7

Introduction 17

Chapter 1: 3 Concrete Steps to Jumpstart Your Job Search 25

    1.1 How Employers Hire 26

    1.2 Join a Users Group 29

        1.2.1 Making the Most of Users' Groups 35

        1.2.2 Making the Most of Online Groups 38

    1.3 Start a Side Project 39

        1.3.1 Using Github 44

        1.3.2 What Makes a Good Side Project? 45

        1.3.3 Making Your Side Project Work 47

    1.4 Update Your Resume 50

        1.4.1 Resume Basics 57

Chapter 2: Why Your Job Search Failed 63

    2.1 Why You're Not Getting Interviews 64

        2.1.1 Entering the Hiring Process Earlier 68

    2.2 You're Not Getting Job Offers 71

    2.3 How to Get Hired 78

        2.3.1 My First Development Job 79

        2.3.2 Becoming a Team Lead: My Second Job 82

        2.3.3 The Job I Turned Down 85

    2.3.4 My Third Full Time Job 87

    2.3.5 My First Client: Going Freelance 90

    2.3.6 My Next Client: A Job Through a Recruiter 91

    2.3.7 And so the Story Goes 92

Chapter 3: Knowing Who to Target - Designing Your Dream Job 95

  3.1 Location 98

    3.1.1 Finding Companies Near You 100

    3.1.2 Finding Remote Jobs 101

  3.2 Salary 103

  3.3 Benefits 106

    3.3.1 Retirement Benefits 108

    3.3.2 Paid Time Off 110

    3.3.3 Other Benefits 111

  3.4 Technology Stack 111

  3.5 Boss 112

  3.6 Co-Workers 114

  3.7 Culture and Corporate Mission 115

  3.8 Job Expectations 118

  3.9 Development Processes 118

  3.10 Opportunities for Growth 120

  3.11 How To Design Your Dream Job: Choosing Your Top 3 "Must Haves" 122

- Chapter 4: Researching Companies 125
  - 4.1 Finding Companies that Match Your Top 3 125
    - 4.1.1 Where to Start 126
  - 4.2 GlassDoor.com 131
    - 4.2.1 Resume and Cover Letter Materials .. 136
  - 4.3 The Company's Website 139
    - 4.3.1 The About Page 141
    - 4.3.2 The Careers Page 145
  - 4.4 Social Media, Blogs, and YouTube 148
  - 4.5 Employees 150
    - 4.5.1 Connecting with Employees 151
    - 4.5.2 What to Ask 152
  - 4.6 LinkedIn 155
- Chapter 5: Resumes that Work 171
  - 5.1 Formatting Your Resume 172
  - 5.2 Example Resume 183
    - 5.2.1 Formatting 183
    - 5.2.2 Contact Information 185
    - 5.2.3 Education 185
    - 5.2.4 Freelancing 187
    - 5.2.5 Work Experience 188
    - 5.2.6 Open Source and Side Projects 190

- 5.2.7 Blog Posts, Podcasts, and Screencasts 191

Chapter 6: Cover Letters 197
- 6.1 The Four Parts of a Cover Letter 200
  - 6.1.1 The Introduction 203
  - 6.1.2 Tell Them Why You Want to Work There 206
  - 6.1.3 Explain Why You're a Great Candidate 209
  - 6.1.4 Invitation to Contact You 212
- 6.2 Other Cover Letter Guidelines 213

Chapter 7: Following Up 215
- 7.1 Email #1 217
- 7.2 Following on Social Media 222
- 7.3 Interacting on Social Media 224
- 7.4 Email #2: A Quick Note 226
- 7.5 Email #3: Did I Miss Something? 228
- 7.6 Alternative Follow Up Methods 230
  - 7.6.1 Postal Mail 231
  - 7.6.2 Going into the Office 233
  - 7.6.3 Phone Calls 235

Chapter 8: Getting Noticed 239
- 8.1 Getting Noticed by Companies You're Targeting 242
  - 8.1.1 Co-working From the Office 243

- 8.1.2 Going into the Corporate Office........245
- 8.1.3 Building Add-ons 247
- 8.1.4 Contributing to Corporate Open Source 249
  - How to Contribute.......................................251
- 8.1.5 Attending Corporate Events 254
- 8.2 Getting Noticed by New Companies.........256
  - 8.2.1 Users' Groups....................................257
    - Meet People..258
    - Help Organize Meetings.............................260
    - Give a Talk...262
    - Start a Users' Group...................................265
  - 8.2.2 Conferences.......................................267
    - Local Conferences......................................269
    - Meet the Speakers 271
    - Attend Workshops......................................276
    - Meet Other Attendees.................................278
    - Approaching Speakers................................284
    - Approaching Sponsors 287
    - Approaching Organizers 289
    - Volunteering...291
    - Conference Speaking 293
  - 8.2.3 Contributing to Open Source.............296
  - 8.2.4 Building a Media Platform................300

General Advice on Building a Media Platform 301

Blogging..304

Podcasting 307

Video 309

8.2.5 Online Communities 310

Be Active...311

Getting Personal Attention 315

8.2.6 Hack Nights and Hackathons 316

Chapter 9: Winning Interviews............................321

9.1 A Few Notes of Caution.............................324

9.2 Phone Screenings 333

9.2.1 Regular Interviews 337

Dress Up One Level 338

Arrive Early...339

Be Confident 340

Be Honest..341

Ask Questions 343

Follow Up 349

9.3 Technical Screenings 350

9.3.1 Coding Sessions 350

Whiteboard Coding 353

9.3.2 Answering Technical Questions.........357

Chapter 10: Salary Negotiations 361

10.1 Know Your Numbers 362

10.2 Make Then Give You the First Number..364

10.3 Making a Counter Offer 366

10.4 Negotiations Are Not Just on Salary 369

10.5 Walking Away 371

Chapter 11: Conclusion 373

11.1 Update Your Resume 373

11.2 Find and Join a Local Users' Group 374

11.3 Start a Side Project 374

11.4 Figure Out What You Want 375

11.5 Research Companies You're Applying To 375

11.6 Stand Out 376

11.7 Send a Customized Resume and Cover Letter to the Company You're Applying To.....376

11.8 Practice for Interviews 377

11.9 Negotiate Your Salary..............................377

11.10 You Can Do This 377

Introduction

Finding a developer job that you'll love sounds like it should be easy. All you need is someone with money who will pay you to write code.

The problem is that every employer and position is a little different. Teams work differently, they expect different things, and the companies prioritize different things. This means that they're all looking for different skills, personalities, and experience levels to make things work when they write software.

To make things worse, companies often don't really know what they want, so they follow the hiring practices of their former bosses and recommendations from Human Resources. This means that if you're new or have some extra hurdles to overcome, it can be extremely difficult to convince them that you can do the job. Furthermore, if they don't know what they want, then they mostly hire on how they feel about you at the end of the interview.

To overcome these problems, programmers looking for a job need to know what they're looking for and how to find companies that match up with what they need. Then, they need to find ways around the traditional hiring model so they can prove themselves without being caught up in the process of checking the boxes for Human Resources and inexperienced hiring managers.

The first chapter has you put into place the things that will put you in the best position to find and take advantage of opportunities to meet people who are looking to hire. The next part of this book will walk you through the process of identifying the "Big Three" things that you should be looking for in potential employers. Then, we'll show you how to find companies that match up with your Big Three. Finally, we'll help you get around the common issues with hiring processes and guide you through negotiating a great salary at the company of your dreams.

Many developers post their resumes to job boards or other job listings and rarely get called in for interviews. Others are able to get interviews, but never get the offer. And, most developers don't even know where to start.

If you're not getting the results you want, you need to try a different job search process.

Our job search process avoids all of the issues you're likely to encounter with the "Spray and Pray" strategy of sending your resume to everyone and hoping they get back to you.

Plus, in the first chapter, it delivers 3 concrete steps to jumpstart your job search.

The author—Charles Max Wood—has been a web developer since 2005. He has used these techniques to find dozens of full-time jobs and remote freelancing clients as a software developer. This process has worked over and over again to find the jobs and clients that he was looking for.

He has also coached dozens of developers into finding jobs they love.

Charles has also worked with many employers to help them find developers that match their needs and has hired a number of developers for projects at Devchat.tv and as a developer team lead at various companies.

Charles is the host of a number of podcasts about software development and has talked to developers, designers, technical managers and thought leaders about both technical topics and soft skills. This requires him to stay up-to-date both in the programming world and the job market.

Many students found jobs within a few weeks of consulting with Charles who had been looking for jobs for 6 months or more. They've built portfolios that demonstrate both what they are capable of and an ongoing commitment to learning. They have also identified companies that provide what they're looking and landed jobs they are still happily working at.

One example is David. David knew that his current job was going to end within a year. He wanted to know what he could do to find companies that needed Project Managers and make the job transition as seamless as possible. After going through Charles' course, he was able to identify the kinds of companies he wanted to work at, topics they were interested in, and began making videos on YouTube discussing Project Management techniques to prepare himself for a successful job search.

Ken is from an area that doesn't have a large, vibrant tech community. Finding a programming job nearby was nearly impossible. After taking this course, he was able to identify the kind of employer he was looking for. He updated his resume and his interview skills, then began focusing his attention on companies he could work for remotely from where he lives.

Our job search process will begin by providing you 3 ways to start your job search that will build the foundation for you to find a great job and allow you to take advantage of any opportunities that come your way while you take the next steps in finding your dream programming job.

It then expands into helping you identify companies that provide the type of job you want. It will show you how to conduct a targeted job search aimed at getting you a job at one of these companies within 2 weeks to 2 months.

It will show you how to build a portfolio that attracts employers and gets you noticed. Then, you'll get a step-by-step walkthrough on meeting people who work for the companies you want, preparing for interviews, and negotiating your salary.

Don't be the typical bootcamp graduate that spends 6 months applying to every job that comes open, becoming frustrated because no one will get back to you. We can shorten this process by helping you level up, build a portfolio, and find companies to apply to that line up with what you your career goals.

Chapter 1: 3 Concrete Steps to Jumpstart Your Job Search

Often, when someone starts looking for a job, opportunities start finding them. Most of the time it's because they start doing things that put them in a position to meet people who work for companies that are hiring. But sometimes, it's just the way things work.

In order to create more of these opportunities and to more easily take advantage of them when they arise, I recommend you immediately begin doing three things:

- Attending a Users Group
- Working on a Side Project
- Updating Your Resume

To explain why, I need to delve briefly into what a job is and how employers hire.

1.1 How Employers Hire

We go into depth in Box 1.3 on how employers find programmers to hire. I'm going to summarize the relevant points for understanding why you need to do these particular things first.

Hiring managers tend to hire the people they can most easily reach. That means hiring people recommended by people they trust and hiring people they meet in life. If they're attending Users' Groups or if they have employees that attend, then being at the Users' Group immediate moves you closer to the person making the hiring decision. Otherwise, you have to send your resume in like everyone else and hope you get picked.

Once they find someone they think they can hire—hopefully, that's you, they have to make sure that you can do the job. This is where your resume, side projects, and interview skills come in. If you have things on your resume that demonstrate that you've done some of the things they need done at work, they're more likely to hire you.

If you have a side projects that has working code in it doing what they need done, you're much more likely to get their attention because they automatically know that you can do whatever it is they need that overlaps with your project.

All three of these things show a certain amount of initiative that is attractive.

For example, imagine that you go to a Users' Group and participate by commenting or asking questions during a presentation. Once that's done, you strike up a conversation with someone else in the room who, during the conversation, tells you that their company is hiring developers. You mention that you'd be happy to send in your resume. They tell you that would be great.

Now, rather than wait until you remember to send it the next day, you have them hold on for a second while you email them the resume on the spot. (This is where having a prepared resume comes in.) Now they have it and if they're excited about you they can immediately forward it to their boss.

You also slip the URL for your side project where you've been working on a Ruby on Rails application with a React front end into the email and ask them to have a look at it while you're at it. (This is where the side project comes in.) Now you have someone who will see what you can do advocating for your hiring with their boss at a company that you can look into to check if they're a good fit for you.

All because you were at a Users' Group with someone who was looking for someone they'd like to work with.

1.2 Join a Users Group

The most effective thing you can do for your job search is to find a group of developers who get together regularly and participate. These groups are set up to help as many people build the kinds of relationships that you're looking for if you're trying to get hired. (They pay off in other ways too, but that's beyond the scope of this book.)

Generally, it's easier to build relationships with potential co-workers and bosses in person. It is possible, however, to do it virtually if you can't find a local meetup.

The first two steps of this process are designed to give you something to show people when they ask about you or interview you. Joining a Users Group is aimed specifically at getting you the opportunity to be introduced, noticed, and interviewed.

Users groups or "meetups" are gatherings of people with a common interest talking about and hearing presentations about related topics. You can find groups about everything from knitting to marathon running. There are programming focused groups all over the world. Many of them are focused on a particular language or framework.

Others are more general and attract all kinds of developers.

The easiest way to find a group is to go to Meetup.com and enter your zip or postal code and search for programming groups in your area. You can search for specific programming languages or frameworks if you're excited about one. If you can't find anything, then broaden your search to "software," "developers," or "programming." If you can't find a group that discusses the technologies you're interested in, go to another software group—even if they're not about your specific interests.

Most of my coaching students protested at this point that they didn't live near a major city and wouldn't have a Users' Group available for them to join. In those cases, I'd search for them on my computer on Meetup.com and list what I found. I only had one student out of dozens who didn't have something nearby that directly addressed his interests. He lived in a fairly small island nation off the South American coast.

So, unless you're in a remote area, you should be able to find something nearby. If you can't find anything nearby, post to some local Facebook groups and search LinkedIn for people nearby stating that you're interested in getting together with people who want to talk about programming. You may be surprised at who you find.

Box 1.1. A Small Rural Users' Group

My friends Miles Forrest and Curtis McHale live the middle of British Columbia about an hour and a half from Vancouver. They're rural enough that it's not trivial for them to drive into town.

In 2014, Miles gave a [talk at Cascadia Ruby Conf](#) where he explains how he runs the Frazier Valley Ruby Brigade.

His basic ideas are to do Hack Nights, have everyone bring a project, and meet every week.

Not everyone who comes is a full time Ruby developer and his group isn't that big. They have a dozen or so people show up, they get companies to send the books and other goodies, and they have great discussions about code in a little cafe in the middle of nowhere.

Hack nights are a great way to start too! No one has to prepare anything and if you're the only person who shows up, you can still have a hack night. You can also meet anywhere that has free WiFi. So, coffee shops, someone's house or office, or a school.

Meeting every week also means that people can come when the are able and if they miss a week or two, it can still work for them.

Finally, you can also reach out to publishing companies for User Group programs and build a library of books. They'll send them to you for free.

Then just show up each week with a paper sign set up on your table with your group's name on it.

I actually did something like this for Entrepreneurs called Co-Working Thursdays and set up a group on Meetup.com. I'm still friends with some of the folks I met there and created some lasting business and personal relationships from it.

For more details on how to put something together like this, I highly recommend you watch Miles' talk.

1.2.1 Making the Most of Users' Groups

Users' Groups are the easiest way to meet people in the industry. In Box 1.3 I mentioned that employers generally start looking for people with the people they know and the people their co-workers know. Attending the Users' Group is a great place to be in these folks' networks.

You can also have a look at the companies the other attendees work for to see if they line up with what you'd like from an employer.

The best ways to get noticed in a Users' Group are to be an organizer, to speak, and to participate.

Being an organizer has nothing to do with your skills as a developer, but people will notice if you're involved in pulling the meetup together. It also doesn't mean that you're the group's original founder. All it means is that you participate in getting the meeting to happen. So, what I recommend is that you go to a couple of the group's meetings, then approach the organizer and see if you can help get the meeting together. You can offer to email out meeting announcements, line up food sponsorships, get books and other swag to share, or approach speakers. All of these are great opportunities to meet other people in the wider community as well.

Speaking isn't everyone's cup of tea, but it's a great way to get you noticed. My first presentation was a 5 minute presentation on Ruby's String class. I walked through some of the methods provided by Ruby for strings and explained how I liked to use them. It wasn't fancy or advanced, but it opened up some discussion and gave me something to talk about with my fellow attendees.

Participation is also key to getting noticed. By raising your hand to ask questions or to share your thoughts, you'll be noticed by the speaker and other attendees. It also shows a desire to learn. It does take a little nerve to put yourself out there, but there is almost no downside to it. The most common thing I hear when recommending this is "What if I ask a dumb question?" The answer is that you're probably not the only one who has that question and even if you are, you're getting the answer from a well informed source who can enlighten the entire group.

Once you've gotten yourself out there—or even before—you can start having conversations with the other attendees.

Find out where they work, what they do, what they're learning, and if their company is hiring. You can also ask them if they're willing to help you with anything you're stuck on in your side project to see if you could get some mentorship.

1.2.2 Making the Most of Online Groups

With online groups, the only visibility you have is through participation. If you want to be noticed there, you have to post often. The best posts you can put up are ones about your side project. So, when you get stuck, need a new library, or want to start expanding your knowledge, post to the group and ask your question.

You can also post when you read a blog post or watch a conference talk and need clarification. The personal interaction can often come in the followup.

Finally, getting noticed often has more to do with other folks than with you. So, find the most popular users of the online group and comment on their posts. If you're consistently responding to a person, they can't help but take notice of you when they come back to respond.

1.3 Start a Side Project

Most people I've coached haven't really thought about what getting a job means beyond getting paid and writing code. If you approach your job search from the standpoint of the company, it changes the feel of your job search. What a company wants is not someone who slings code. It's more complicated than that.

Companies want people who can solve their problems and collaborate with the other people in the company to do it.

Your resume does the job of telling them that you can solve their problems and your cover letter lets them know how you think you'll fit in. The trick is having something to put in your resume and to talk about in your interview.

Box 1.2. I got laid off and hired in the same day

After working at my first programming job for about 1 year, the General Manager called me in. The contract I had been working on their behalf had ended and they had shopped me to their only other Ruby on Rails based client the previous week. He had just heard back.

Bad news! That other client had looked at my resume and had decided that I didn't have enough experience for them to take a chance on me. That despite the guarantees from my boss and from the other Ruby on Rails developer from that company who had been working with them for the last 6 months redesigning their entire operation from start to finish.

This company had said that they usually benched people for a couple weeks when there was a shortage of work they could do and one of the partners had a list of IT tasks I was qualified to handle, so I expected to be splitting my time over the next 2 weeks learning .NET or Java to pick up another project in that technology and the IT tasks.

Nope! I got laid off.

Believe me, that's a phone call you don't want to make to your wife. Especially when you have 2 kids. Oh! And did I mention that it was our third wedding anniversary?!

I got home around 11 in the morning and decided to send my resume around to a bunch of places since the rest of my day was suddenly free until that evening when we were planning to go out to dinner. (*I call sending resumes out like this "Spray and Pray" and have since learned much better ways to find a job, which is in this book.*)

It turned out that a local company was looking on one of the job listing platforms not long after I blasted my resume all over the place and called me to set up an interview. Since I had the afternoon free, we set up the interview for around 4pm.

During the interview, I talked a bit about what I had done for the 2 clients I had worked for at my previous employer, the side projects I worked on at the employer before that, and my video series <u>Teach Me To Code</u> that walked through various Ruby on Rails features. We also talked about what they were looking for and discussed a couple of their upcoming projects.

As I was driving home from the interview to pick up my wife for dinner, I got a phone call from the manager who had interviewed me. They were offering me a job and asked when I could start.

I went to my new job the next morning.

Once you get to the interview, you'll want to have something to talk to them about. Usually, they'll dive into what you've done. This essentially translates neatly into your job experience as a software developer.

The funny thing is that many employers have figured out that the truly exceptional developers are the ones who are learning on their own and coding outside of work. Plus, if you're new and don't have job experience, then you need to be able to discuss experience that comes from beyond job experience.

This is where having a side project comes in.

1.3.1 Using Github

If you don't have one yet, go set up an account on Github.

Github is the largest collection of open source software anywhere and is a place where software developers at most levels store their code. It's also an easy place for interested employers to go see what code you're writing. Though, admittedly, most won't go to the trouble, the ones that do are generally more interested in getting higher caliber developers and are therefore better places to work.

It's also got a contributions tracker that people can look at that lets them know how active you are in working on your side projects, open source, and other public projects on Github.

1.3.2 What Makes a Good Side Project?

A good side project has two primary attributes. First, it's something you're interested in building or working on. Second, it gives you the opportunity to experiment with technologies you want to learn, learn better, or demonstrate expertise in.

I've coached several people who were looking for jobs that felt like they needed to build one of the "standard projects" to show what they could do. The most popular of these in the communities I work in are blog platforms, twitter clones, and chat rooms.

The problems with these particular standard projects are that there are many tutorials out there on how to build these. That means that they often get discounted as a demonstration of your ability to follow a tutorial instead of a real showcase of your capability as a developer. They're also not usually aligned with your interests as well as other projects might be.

To pick a solid side projects, I generally recommend that you think about your hobbies, interests, or problems outside of software development and then build something that addresses those. Then, go look at the companies you want to work for or think about the technologies you want to find a job working with and start the project using those.

You don't have to finish them or publish them. Just having them and having something to work on is the main idea.

I've had a number of people who were really into finances build budgeting apps. I, personally, love Boy Scouts, so I've started a few advancement trackers that I've never finished. Others have built systems to track their collections of different types of collectables. Just find something that fits you.

1.3.3 Making Your Side Project Work

Once you have your side project worked out, then you're ready to make it something you want to reference on your resume and give you something to discuss in interviews.

Above anything else, make sure you contribute to the project as many days as you can. That contributions tracker on Github turns the day green when you make a contribution. The more contributions or commits you make, the darker it gets. The reason this is so important is that it shows your commitment to learning and growing. It also demonstrates that you love coding and that you practice at least a little every day. Practice is key to improving at anything.

At least once per week, make sure that you're taking on something that you don't know how to do. This will push you to grow and give you a chance to ask others for help or to figure out how to solve the problem with some help from the internet. Today's applications are being built to do things that software has never done before. That doesn't mean we never have commonly structured problems. Instead, it means that no developer knows exactly how to solve every problem they'll encounter as part of their job.

Lastly, keep your README file up to date. This is the first place people will look when evaluating your project. It should include your email address and a link to your resume. Link to any blog posts or other media you create talking about what you're learning. It should also include setup instructions so someone can run it on their computer and an explanation of what it does and how it's designed.

We'll talk in more detail about Side Projects in Chapter cha:side_projects

1.4 Update Your Resume

Once you get noticed at a Users' Group or other venue, a natural segue will come up where you can share that you're looking for a job. This usually comes up as "Where do you work?" or "How long have you been a developer?" At that point, you can reply with "I just graduated from bootcamp and I'm looking for a job." or something similarly appropriate to your situation.

Most people are happy to help each other, so you can then ask them if they know of any job openings. If the company they work for is hiring or if they know someone who works at a company who is hiring, you can ask if you can email them your resume.

Having an updated resume makes preparing and sending a resume a lot easier. You will still want to edit your resume to accentuate the areas that that company says they're interested in. You'll also want to prepare your cover letter to present yourself as the kind of person that others at that company will want to work with.

One other area that this helps in is the sort of impromptu interview that sometimes occurs, where someone will ask what you've done with a particular technology or if you have experience working with tools or processes the company uses. Having broken that information out into your resume is a

Box 1.3. Don't Spray and Pray

The conventional wisdom in job searches is a method I call "Spray and Pray." It goes something like this.

Step one, pull together an up to date resume with a bunch of information about how you've done as much cutting edge stuff as you can defend in a face-to-face interview.

Step two, take this resume to as many job boards as you can find in a Google search in 15 minutes.

Step three, any job listed on those job boards that look remotely interesting to you, gets your new resume sent to them. This is the "spray" part of the method.

Step four, go to any interviews that come from spraying your resume all over the internet. Hoping for these interviews is the "pray" portion since you're relying on luck that your resume reflects what the company wants or that few people applied, this giving you a chance.

Step five, get a job offer that you're willing to accept.

There are several problems with this method. Let me address the two largest.

First, your resume is too generic. You may actually have the skills and temperament that the company is looking for. However, since you're sending around a resume that only has the basic information you think some definition of "people" or "bosses" want, you may leave something off or fail to emphasize something that would get you hired.

Second, you're playing to all the weaknesses in the process employers use to find people. Just like you're hoping *someone* will hire you, once a company exhausts the most effective ways of finding good employees, they start looking for *someone* they can hire. The problem is that *someone* isn't very specific.

Employers follow a general process for finding new employees. This isn't a well thought out process, it's really a very natural one.

The first thing they do is talk to their employees and let them know that they're going to expand the team or start a new team or project. The really smart employers actually take this opportunity to go to their top performers and see if they know other top performers they can recruit. But, even if they don't do this, their employees generally will talk to anyone they'd like to work with about applying.

If no one the employees know come on board, then they start going to places they've successfully recruited top performers from in the past. This means that they may go to a meetup or Users' Group. Or they may go to an online forum or mailing list. Or even to a university or other institution that's worked out for them.

Once that fails, they'll talk to their friends outside of these groups.

Then, they list the job on job boards or hire a recruiter. This is where you come in with your resume spraying. If there are enough people looking—and there are, especially for junior developer positions—they'll wind up with dozens of resumes.

Did I mention that these people are already busy? When they get a lot of resumes, they're looking for any reason to rule someone out. So, if you don't have something on there that compels them to call you, you're basically betting that everyone else who applied has less experience or less relevant skills than you. And, with a generic resume, that's a long bet.

So, why do you write up your basic resume? It's like preparing a speech. When someone asks you about what you've done, you know your talking points. It also allows you to respond quickly when asked for a resume by having something you can start from before doing a little research and adding in what you've done that the company will want.

1.4.1 Resume Basics

Your resume is essentially an easy to consume listing of the things you'd like your potential employer to know about you. HR departments and hiring managers usually only scan resumes, so make it easy to follow. It's also usually somewhat limited to things that you've done, but there are a few things that you want to make sure are on there an easy to find.

The primary thing they need to be able to find is your contact information. The resume's job is to get you a job interview and you can't get a job interview without them reaching out to you in some way. So, put this at the top in a slightly bigger font than the rest of the information on your resume.

The other things you want are there are the things that show the hiring manager that you can do the job and that you're the kind of person they want to hire. For experienced developers, this is nearly always their job history. For non-experienced developers, it's their relevant job history along with any side projects they have that demonstrate expertise.

You can also reference blog posts, podcast episodes, YouTube videos, and conference talks that you've made that demonstrate that you understand and can communicate ideas about software to other people.

Essentially, the point here is that you put your resume in the following order:

1. Contact information
2. Relevant work experience

3. Relevant education, bootcamps, and certifications
4. Open source contributions
5. Side projects
6. Other work experience

If you're wondering about your other work experience, keep in mind that it does tell them the kind of employee you've been to date and what kinds of things you're good at outside of coding. So, if you have room on your resume, make sure to include this information.

Also remember that you don't need to have a Computer Science degree or a genius IQ. You just need to be able to solve problems your employer has or be able to figure it out.

For more formatting and ideas of what to put into your resume, go check out Chapter 5.

One other thing, if you can, include a cover letter.

Sometimes there's no time to write a cover letter. However, most of the time, it's helpful to include one that gives the HR departments and hiring managers an idea of the type of person you are and how enthusiastic or committed you are to learning what you need to learn to do the job. A lot of these "soft skills" and personal attributes are tricky to communicate in a resume, but are crucial to making a decision based on how you'll fit into a team or company.

When writing a cover letter, spend 15 minutes looking through the company's website and social media to get a feel for the type of company they are and what sort of corporate culture they have. Then you can specifically address the things they say are important to them while also building yourself up as someone who would be happy there and someone they'd like to have around. We'll have more about cover letters in Chapter 5.

Chapter 2: Why Your Job Search Failed

While preparing for this book and its accompanying video course, I interviewed dozens of developers who were stuck in their job search. Most of them were trying to get their first or second coding job. The rest either lived in places where there wasn't a strong tech community or had some reason for wanting or needing a remote job.

In nearly every case, they were following the generally accepted pattern for finding a job:

1. Build your resume
2. Search job listings online
3. Send your resume to anything that looks promising

4. Go to any interviews that come up
5. Wait for a job offer

Usually, they'd get stuck either waiting for interviews, or, if they got interviews, waiting for job offers. None would come.

The remote folks more often got stuck on even knowing where to begin since most job listings are location based and require you to be nearby.

2.1 Why You're Not Getting Interviews

If you're not getting interviews, it's probably happening for one of two reasons. Either the person in charge of hiring is too busy or your resume doesn't help you stand out. Of course, both of these stem from an unseen problem.

You're entering the hiring process at the same point as everyone else.

Let's back up and talk about the first problem. The person in charge of hiring is too busy.

When an employer starts looking for someone to hire, it's usually because their workload doesn't match the number of developers they need to get it done. And because they're busy trying to fill the gaps, unless a good candidate appears in front of them, it's likely they'll put off the next steps of the hiring process. Then, when they're desperate, they'll list the job.

A job listing will generally get a lot of resumes—especially in a competitive market or a large city. This means that they face the huge task of sorting through a big pile of resumes. So, they'll either put it off, or they'll get through enough resumes to line up some interviews with a few promising candidates and ignore the rest of the pile. In either case, unless you're on top of they pile, you won't get called in for an interview even with the best resume.

The second scenario stems from the number of responses the employer gets from the job listing. Unless you're one of the top 5 to 10 candidates in the pile, you're probably not going to get called. It's not necessarily how good your resume is, but how good it is compared to the rest of the pile.

Now, before you throw up your hands in frustration over the length or quality of your resume, let's talk briefly about what makes a "good" resume.

Your resume's job is to get you an interview. The way it does that is by showing the person reading the resume that you're the kind of person they want to hire. It demonstrates that you have the skills they want and that you're a good fit for the team and the company—both culturally and technically. The point being that a good resume for one company will be different from a good resume for another company.

So, if you spend a few minutes researching the company and then update your resume to reflect what you know about them, you may be able to outshine better qualified candidates.

We cover researching companies in Chapter 4, building resumes that work in Chapter 5, and filling in the gaps with cover letters in Chapter 6.

2.1.1 Entering the Hiring Process Earlier

You can mitigate the issues surrounding busy hiring managers and subpar resumes by getting to know people in the community, the company, and participating in any way you can.

In the case of the overwhelmed manager, you need to enter the hiring process earlier. Get on the manager's radar through other channels and convince them that you can alleviate some of the overload they're dealing with. As for your resume's quality, getting on the radar early means that you're only competing with anyone else who enters at the same stage you did instead of the other job seekers looking at the same job boards you are.

You see, there's a certain progression to a job search that naturally occurs. When a hiring manager needs to hire someone, the most natural place to go is to people they already know who can do the job. One team I was hired onto had mostly been together through 3 different companies because their manager had changed jobs twice and had hired people from his old teams as positions had opened up. This is a natural way for a manager to go because they already know what they're getting.

Once the manager's own network is exhausted, then he or she goes to their team's network. That's how I got hired onto that particular team. I was friends with a developer named David who was talking about his job and mentioned that they were looking for developers. I was ready to move on from my current job, so I applied and got hired.

In fact, the manager who hired me told me that my resume wasn't deep enough and that he almost didn't hire me. However, they were only considering one other person who had disqualified himself. So, since David vouched for me and because I showed some initiative, he gave me a chance. Needless to say, I went out of my way to make sure it paid off for him.

When the manager's and team's networks fail, they'll go to other communities they belong to. The easiest way for them to do this is on message boards, chat channels, and forums. They may also go to or send employees to a Users' Group where they can mention that they're hiring.

These are the areas you need to operate in. This book walks you through building your resume and then how to leverage these layers of the job search to get noticed before the company lists your job on the job board.

2.2 You're Not Getting Job Offers

Once you've got someone's attention and get invited to an interview, your new objective is to demonstrate that you're their only choice—or at least an easy choice.

Keep in mind that there is a lot of pre-judgement that goes on in the hiring manager's head. When you go in for an interview, you're competing with both the other candidates and the interviewer's impression of you based on what's in your resume and anything else they've come across.

If you're at the top of the pack, it's your job to lose—usually because you fail to live up to the expectations they have going into the interview. It can also happen if someone blows the interviewer's initial impressions of them out of the water.

We have a whole chapter on interviewing in Chapter 9 but let me point out some of the things you can start doing now while you work on lining up your next interview.

Interviewing is a skill. You increase your skill in anything by practicing. Make friends with senior developers and team leads and then ask them to sit down and do mock interviews with you. One terrific place to do this is after a Users' Group meeting. If you can't find a local group, find an online forums where you can find someone who will practice with you over a video chat.

Have them take notes on what you could do better and what skills they're looking for in that job that you could improve on.

Also, while interviewing be confident. Tell them what you know and how you know it. This is where side projects come in if you don't have actual coding job experience.

Finally, be honest. I've interviewed hundreds of people for jobs. In every case, I ask questions until I get an honest "I don't know." The reason is that if someone is going to lie to me about what they know, then I can't trust them to get help when they need it. Besides, if I can accurately assess where you are, then I can put you in a position where you'll succeed.

Box 2.1. My First Development Job Interview

My first development job interview stands out for me. I'm not sure if it's because of how nervous I was or because I somehow got the job.

I had been applying to Quality Assurance Engineer jobs for about a month. This was mainly due to the fact that I had been doing Q.A.—software testing—for about 6 months and had run the Customer Support team for my employer for about a year and a half before that. I knew Q.A. but wanted to be a developer. So, I applied to a development job I saw listed.

They called me in for an interview primarily because my past jobs included various server and network administration jobs. They were a software consultancy that needed someone to help with those jobs when they weren't working on client projects.

I walked into their office in a shirt and tie and sat down with the General Manager. That part of the interview is mostly a blur to me now. He mainly wanted to make sure that I'd fit with their way of doing things.

Then, we went into the other room and he called the company's only other Ruby on Rails developer to conduct the technical end of the interview. The interview was by phone because he was home for his daughter's 8th birthday party. It also meant that I didn't have a good read on what he thought of the interview while it was ongoing.

After talking through the basics of Ruby on Rails, he asked me if knew what Design Patterns were.

Of course, I had no idea. So, I said so. "No, I don't know what they are."

He gave me a basic rundown and asked me if I understood. I responded that I did and then gave an example from my experience working with Ruby on Rails.

He asked me about testing Rails.

I responded with a couple of things I had experimented with and then provided him with the obligatory "I dunno" when he probed deeper.

The interview went back and forth like that for about 45 minutes. He'd quickly reach the lack of depth in my knowledge and then explain what I was missing.

When it was finally over, I walked out of there knowing I had completely blown the interview. I didn't know anything they needed me to know.

I got the job offer the next day.

It turned out that I had a passable knowledge of the basics of Ruby on Rails and the ability to recognize principles and patterns when they were shown to me. I also had demonstrated a complete willingness to learn. All that coupled with a time crunch the company was under to fill their client's needs meant that I got the job and a lot of on-the-job training.

You don't need to be a code genius. You just have to be able to show them that you can get the job done!

Now that we've jumped into why your job searches have failed, let's get you started with things that will help you right away, then go down the path of doing targeted searches, getting noticed, and having successful interviews.

2.3 How to Get Hired

Getting hired is a strange combination of standing out, being the right candidate, and timing. We've already talked about timing and getting on someone's radar early in the process before the job gets listed. But let's talk about how people actually get hired as software developers.

Let me start with my experience getting hired as a developer and as a contractor. You should be able to see a progression in the ways I've found work. I can tell you that the methods I used to find work later in my career were much more effective than those used at the beginning.

This book is designed to show you how to get jobs in the most effective way—the way I did later in my career and as a freelancer. My later contracts and jobs came almost exclusively through people I knew, podcasts I hosted, and videos I created.

2.3.1 My First Development Job

The first full time software developer job I had, I got while looking for a Quality Assurance job. I applied to a software consultancy who was looking for a Ruby on Rails developer to help on one of their client projects. Since I had been doing Ruby on Rails on internal side projects at my previous job I had the kind of experience they needed and was a new enough programmer that they didn't need to pay me as much as their senior developers.

In this case, I failed at standing out in any way that got me the interview. They didn't find me because of anything I did.

I just applied online and managed to get in for an interview. It was at the interview that I stood out as someone who could pick things up quickly and had enough skills to deliver for the client under the mentorship of a more senior developer.

I also stood out because I had 5 years of part-time experience at Brigham Young University as a systems administrator working in the university's datacenter while I got my Computer Engineering degree. I was also the only candidate they interviewed who had a college degree in a computer related field. My next two jobs were the ones where I stood out for other reasons that got me the interview and, ultimately, the job.

In other words, I was the right candidate because they could pay me what they wanted to and I had enough qualifications in other areas to make me attractive. They were also in a hurry to hire someone for the job I got, so they didn't interview many people. In fact, the day I got a call from the General Manager offering me the job, I got another call from him 2 hours later asking me to quit my current job that Friday and to start the next Monday.

The confluence of timing, skill, personality, and experience worked out for me. Timing because they needed someone immediately. The rest came down to my experience building an internal application in Ruby on Rails and having a lot of experience in server and network setup and maintenance—which was sorely needed.

What I can pass on to you from this particular experience is three lessons:

- Learn some non-conventional skills. Devops is a terrific option.
- Apply for jobs you're not sure you're qualified for.
- Demonstrate what you know and an eagerness to learn the rest.

2.3.2 Becoming a Team Lead: My Second Job

After I had been at my first full time developer job for about a year, the client I was working for started cutting costs. They cut my contract and my employer laid me off. During that year with my first employer, I started podcasting and screencasting about Ruby on Rails.

I still only had one year and one job under my belt as a full time developer, though.

I went home and applied to a few jobs on Monster.com. I got called for an interview that afternoon. In this case, I stood out. I had updated my resume to show the work I had done for the consultancy I had worked for before as well as my screencasts and podcasts.

The screencasts did the trick. The developer who was doing the hiring looked up my screencasts on the internet and watched a few. The interview was pretty short and I got a phone call on the way home asking me when I could start. I went to work for them the next day.

The company was starting two new projects that week and I wound up taking the lead on the team I was placed on soon after joining the company. This was a function of being the most experienced with Ruby on Rails and the company's knowledge of what I had done in the past due to the videos.

I got a raise for being the team lead and was put in a position where I could learn a good deal about both development and leadership. In this case, I learned:

- Keep learning.
- Share what you know.
- Be willing to step up and help where needed.

This company also sent me to my first RubyConf. It was a place to grow and find solutions to problems I hadn't encountered before.

2.3.3 The Job I Turned Down

Eventually, I got tired of my boss at that last job for a number of reasons not relevant to this book.

By this time, I had taken an active role speaking at the local Users' Groups and was fairly well known in the local development community. I started applying to companies my friends were working at—especially companies that seemed to have all the smart people working at them.

One company in particular had several of my friends working there. They also had a large number of conference speakers and frequently sponsored the local programming events. They cared and it showed.

Since I had met the boss and several of the developers on the team at the Users'

Group, I was excited to be interviewing for that job. I had gotten to be good friends with one of their developers in particular, who lived about 2 blocks from me.

I went in for the interview and aced it. We did some pair programming, talked about what I was doing with my screencasts, my work for my current employer, and what I aspired to be doing. They fully supported everything I was working on and encouraged me to come contribute to what they were doing.

I got a job offer later that week. I took it home, thought and prayed about it. Initially, I had an inclination to accept the offer, but had a nagging suspicion that not everything over there was the way I thought it was. I talked to my friend—the one who was my neighbor as well—about it. It turned out that there was a bit of dysfunction going on, but nothing that couldn't be overcome.

I trusted my gut and declined their offer, even though by this time I was suffering at my current job.

Two months later, they laid off all but 3 of their developers. The moral of the story? Trust your gut.

2.3.4 My Third Full Time Job

A few months after turning down the job with that company, my neighbor was talking up how great his new job was. They were doing PHP development, but were going to be doing a transition to Ruby on Rails and he was looking for Rails developers to join the team and help the effort.

He helped me apply and got me an interview, but couldn't promise me a job because I only had 2 years of software development experience under my belt at that point.

When I arrived at the interview, I sat down with my friend and another developer from the development team. We talked for about a half hour about Rails and about what the company was doing. Then I sat down with the development team's manager.

He told me right away that my two years of full time experience was a little less than he wanted. He was excited to see that I had experience leading a team through a few things that the team at this company was looking to change— specifically Agile development practices and setting up continuous integration. Furthermore, my experience setting up and running servers was helpful because the IT team was extremely busy and couldn't always solve those sorts of problems for the development team.

Once again, the timing was right. But this time I had the inside track. I knew that they were switching to Rails because I had been told they were.

I was the right candidate because I had demonstrated my knowledge of what they needed both through the podcasts and screencasts as well as through my explanation of what I had done at my previous job. I could also speak intelligently with the other developers on the team familiar with the experience they were interested in.

The only way I really stood out was that I had a good friend at the company who vouched for me. I was never told that his prompting was why I got the job, but I was told when I was offered the job that I was too new for my new boss to be completely comfortable hiring me—essentially that I was on some sort of probation—and that he was hiring me because I had other skills they needed and he'd had some assurance that I would work out.

By the time I got laid off 6 months later, I was one of the "senior developers" on the team.

2.3.5 My First Client: Going Freelance

When I got laid off by last full time employer, I had worked at 3 jobs that I had loved that had either changed into something that I didn't like or had been laid off. The job that changed and the other job that turned out to be a nightmare, were the ones that had tried every trick they had to get me to stay. One actually threatened to sue me.

I wasn't sure I could find a job that I'd love, so I decided to take a chance at freelancing. It was freelancing that taught me how to find jobs that I'd love and how to get those jobs to find me.

Initially, when I found my first client, I was looking for another full time job while I was looking for clients. I interviewed with them assuming they were hiring full time and wound up consulting with them. I found out later that several of the team members at that company were fans of my screencasts.

2.3.6 My Next Client: A Job Through a Recruiter

The next client I found came through a recruiter that I got connected to through a fan of my podcast. As a general rule, I'm not a fan of recruiters because most of them will do whatever it takes to get developers into interviews—even if they have no shot at getting hired—which winds up wasting a lot of people's time.

This recruiter was different in that he specialized in Ruby on Rails and that he had a client who needed a part time contractor to maintain their website and add features to it on occasion. This turned out to be perfect for me as it got me a long term client and allowed me to cultivate other contracting opportunities.

Again, a referral through my podcasts.

2.3.7 And so the Story Goes

Most of the rest of my clients came through the podcasts or screencasts. Many of them wound up clicking the

"Hire Me" badge I put on my website. Others called my phone number which was also prominently placed on that same badge.

All in all, I wound up getting around the regular hiring process by putting myself out there and then being easy to contact. Try giving a conference talk, Users' Group talk, or writing a blog post and putting your phone number in it if people want to hire you.

Chapter 3: Knowing Who to Target - Designing Your Dream Job

Now that you've taken the steps to prepare your resume, start a side project, and find a group to join, let's get going with your actual job search.

The way you get hired is by standing out. This is why the "Spray and Pray" method of finding a job—the way most people are told to look for a job—doesn't work. You can't stand out if you're sending the same document to the same people as everyone else and hoping what you said is what they want.

Instead, you're more likely to be able to find a job if you target companies you want to work for and then do the work to represent yourself as the kind of person they want to hire.

When most developers are asked what type of job they want or what expectations they have of a company they work for, they often will list some technologies they want to use and may mention that they'd like a paycheck. If you don't have many options, you may have to settle for something that is nearby and pays well.

Most developers, however, have enough mobility to move near to or already live near a tech scene that will support them with a job. In those cases, it becomes a question of which companies to target, because if you're going to go out of your way to get noticed by companies, you may as well work on the ones you want to work at.

And, that's the major question for this chapter: How do I decide which companies to target with my job search?

When answering these questions, keep in mind any things you liked or didn't like about past employers that fit into the upcoming categories.

Also keep in mind that you're not going to find a job that meets every criteria in every area. You'll have to determine which things are most important to you. For example, if you or a family member have a chronic health condition, then your health benefits may be critical. If you're young and in good health, you may be more concerned with the company's culture and how you fit in with your co-workers. In other words, answer all these questions to the extent that you care about them, then prioritize the ones you can't afford to compromise on.

3.1 Location

If you want a job that you go to every day, the location is something you need to consider.

If you're going to work remotely, this matters less for your day-to-day, but international arrangements can have an effect on how you get paid, benefits you receive, and other factors. So, the company's location can impact you as well.

Think about how far or how long you're willing to drive to get to work every day. You will probably come up with two numbers. One for how long your longest ideal commute would be. And, how far you're willing to go before it's not worth it.

Also consider these questions:

- Does it need to be near major roads or highways?
- Is it near another location you'll need to go to every day like a child's school or parent's house?
- Does it need to be near restaurants to eat at? Or will you be bringing food with you every day?
- Do you live near a state or national border? Does it matter what state, country, or currency you're paid in?
- If you're going to move to be near the company, do you need a visa or other documents?

3.1.1 Finding Companies Near You

Finding companies in a particular area is actually relatively easy. LinkedIn searches provide you with tools to find software developers within a certain area. Just log in (or create an account) and click the Search field then click Jobs. Under "All Filters" you can find an option for Location. You can type in a city near you and see what comes up. When I was writing this book, I entered both "Salt Lake City, Utah" and "Provo, Utah" and it allowed me to search near both.

Make a note of which companies are listed. You can apply through LinkedIn, but I recommend you hold off for now. We'll come back around to getting their attention in future chapters of the book.

If you don't get enough results on the Jobs search or want to see what else is out there, try changing to a People search. (Just click the Search bar again and then click "People.") Click "Location" and enter your location like we did for the "Jobs" search. Then use the "All Filters" option to set the Industries to "Computer Software."

Most people's listings show their job title and company in the search results. My "People" search yielded Ancestry, Xactware, Lingotek, and White Canyon Software.

3.1.2 Finding Remote Jobs

If a company has hired remote in they past, they'll likely do it again.

For remote jobs, I find that the "People" search works better for this. You can narrow the search by adding "remote" to the "Title" filter in the search and removing any Location filters you may have added. You may also need to browse through the local search list for companies you don't recognize as local since most people don't list their position as remote in their job title.

It's also useful to look over the job boards for remote jobs. Some of them like <u>WeWorkRemotely</u> list only remote jobs. Just keep in mind that by the time they've listed the job, the companies are getting several resumes and you'll have to work harder to stand out.

Honestly, your best bet is to meet someone who works remotely and then target the company they work for.

You may also want to evaluate whether or not you're willing to work remotely as a contractor and then do a full time job search again when your contract ends.

3.2 Salary

Salary is the one aspect of a development job that every job seeker should have in mind. You should know how much you'd like to make and you should know how much your minimum salary requirement is. A minimum salary is probably going to be a certain percentage higher than your last salary and should at least cover your monthly expenses.

How much you'd like to make is most likely based on what you think you can get, is higher than your last development job—if this isn't your first one&—and should be reasonably close to market rates. This gets a little complicated because we generally don't discuss our salaries with other people, so most developers don't have a good idea what the going market rate is for someone at their level.

One way to find out the market rate for the job you want is to go to Glassdoor. Click on "Salaries" at the top and enter "Software Developer" and your location into the form. This will tell you the average salary for developers in your area. My experience is that brand new developers make about 25% less than what's listed there. Very experienced developers can make 20% or more above that number. Glassdoor also offers an estimation tool if you want to go that route.

Box 3.1. Glassdoor.com

The reason I recommend you look on Glassdoor.com for salary information is because they base their information on what people report to them rather than on surveys, interviews, or other information. Instead, people submit their salary and other information to Glassdoor in exchange for being able to use Glassdoor's database to get information on companies.

Glassdoor also collects information about job interviews at companies, reviews of companies by employees, and other information that we'll use in later chapters to research those companies.

Whatever numbers you come up with, stand firm on your minimum. If a company doesn't pay up to your minimum, then don't apply. If you don't think you can get what you want from one company and you think you can from another, then put more effort into getting noticed by the company that will give you what you want.

I also recommend that you prioritize the aspects of a job that'll make you happy, like co-workers or work environment, then salary, then everything else. If you're not sure what to prioritize because this is your first programming job, prioritize salary and keep in mind that your first job will help you figure out what you should be prioritizing instead.

3.3 Benefits

Benefits come in all kinds. There are health and insurance benefits, retirement benefits, days off, corporate programs, corporate cars, and all kinds of other things. The most commonly discussed are the time off, retirement, and health benefits.

Health insurance is the biggie when we talk about benefits. A lot of people just want to be covered. Other people want a specific kind of plan with certain types of coverage.

There are all kinds of reasons for the kinds of health plans offered by a company. If you're relatively healthy and less likely to use your health coverage beyond a yearly checkup, then you probably don't care as much about the health plan. If you or a family member are ill, you're more likely to care.

If you're in the prior group, just make sure you get a plan that'll cover catastrophes (on the level of cancer or major surgeries) at the very least.

If you're in the latter group, then look over the plan and determine where it fails to cover what you need. You can also sometimes talk to an independent insurance agent and have them estimate your out-of-pocket costs for a particular plan. Then you can figure out if you need a higher salary to go on a particular type of plan.

Finally, if you're in the stage of life where you're having children, maternity coverage is a consideration as well.

Most other benefits are nice to have, but probably won't make or break your dream job. You may think you need them, but on things like retirement, sick and vacation days, and other benefits and perks, you can make up the difference by getting more on your salary and then negotiating for or buying those benefits yourself.

Here are a few more thoughts on the other big benefits people care about.

3.3.1 Retirement Benefits

Retirement benefits are an interesting benefit to consider. This generally becomes more important to people as they get older, but is something that everyone should be considering since the sooner you start saving for retirement, the larger your retirement account will be when you need it.

Retirement plans come in a few different flavors. There are self-funded accounts, some with company matching contributions and some without, and there are company funded accounts.

You should only prioritize this particular benefit if you don't have the discipline to contribute to a retirement account of your own. Companies that match retirement funds are a nice perk, but you can't spend retirement funds until you retire and your investment options are usually better if you contribute to a fund you set up as opposed to one that a company sets up for you, so you don't gain much by making this something you bargain hard for.

3.3.2 Paid Time Off

Paid time off is one of the most lifestyle dependent benefits to consider along with corporate culture and some opportunities for growth. If you like to take vacations, need time off to take care of family, or do lots of volunteer work, then you may care a lot about vacation days. Sick days also comes into play if you have health problems you need to attend to.

You also generally get more vacation days if you're a more senior developer. This is also something you can negotiate when you're negotiating your job offers.

3.3.3 Other Benefits

Other benefits may include:
- Dental Insurance
- Cafeterias
- Gym Memberships
- Corporate Discounts and Partnerships
- Company Car (usually provided to corporate officers and sales people if provided)

These are typically not important enough to make one of your top priorities and can be difficult to negotiate for if the company doesn't already offer them.

3.4 Technology Stack

There are a lot of technology choices out there. Many developers have a set of technologies they like to work with. Others are more flexible in some areas than in others. For the most part, if the languages and frameworks you want to use are or have been part of the mainstream in the last ten years or so, you can very likely find a job working with them.

The level to which you can dictate the technologies you work with also depend on the market you're looking for a job in. Some of the smaller markets only have companies that are building software in widely used technologies like .NET or Java. This may drive you to look for a remote job or consider moving depending on your job market.

3.5 Boss

This is one area that you don't have to have worked as a developer or held a full-time job to know a little about. If you've ever had a job, you've had a boss. You can probably also think of some things you liked or didn't like about that boss. Take a few minutes to consider which bosses you thrived under and which ones you hated working for. What attributes did they have? What approaches to work and assigning work did they have?

Also, consider how you work. Do you prefer to be given large tasks and the freedom to break them down and figure out how to approach them on your own? Or, do you want your boss to give you more fine-grained instructions? Do you want your boss around more? or less? Are you looking for a coach? or just someone who keeps things humming along with minimal involvement?

One of my favorite bosses was involved in the weekly planning and sat down with us to set goals each quarter. He also attached bonuses to those goals to encourage us to continue to grow. But, when it came to the day-to-day programming, he was fairly hands off, knowing that we had planned out what needed to be done that week in our planning meeting and that we'd discuss anything we failed in an agile retrospective at the end of the week.

3.6 Co-Workers

What kind of co-workers do you want? Do you need to feel like you're part of a team or in a club? Do you want to work with people who are smarter or better than you? Are you looking for mentorship? Are you looking to be a mentor? Do you want a group that goes out for lunch regularly? does learning sessions together? or goes out for drinks after work?

3.7 Culture and Corporate Mission

For a lot of people, the corporate culture is a critical element of their workplace. This is more than just whether the company lets you wear shorts or even has a corporate dress code. A friend of mine worked at a company that had a kegerator in the office and a culture of working late and going out for beers after dinner. It's a fun lifestyle if you like beer and don't have a family to go home to. Another company I know of values the "stability of people with families and children." They make their people go home by 5pm every evening and arrange corporate events with bounce houses and water slides.

What matches up with what you want?

Similarly with the company's stated mission. Many companies are about making a difference in a particular field or on a specific social issue. Does this matter to you? Or are you more interested in solving hard or interesting problems for a profitable company? Neither is wrong. But, one may make you happier than another.

Box 3.2. Making a difference isn't changing the world

When I worked for Mozy running their support department, I felt like I was making a difference even though we were a for profit company that didn't address any social issues. This stemmed primarily from the idea that I'd be really upset if I lost my pictures of my kids. So, every time we helped some grandmother get her pictures backed up or some small business get their records backed up, I felt great because I was saving them potential problems and heartache down the road.

One other thing that plays a role here is the vision the company's leaders have for the company. Are they trying to raise venture capital? Are they looking for someone to eventually acquire the company? Do they plan to go public? Is it a small privately held company with plans to remain privately held? Who is the majority owner of the company? Who is on the board? What are they trying to accomplish?

3.8 Job Expectations

We've already talked about some of these issues like when you show up and leave and if the team or company hangs out around work. Besides that, some teams have certain expectations around how and how much you contribute to the company's software.

Some companies expect that you contribute a certain number of features, stories, story points, lines of code, or other measures of productivity.

You may also be expected to be around for specific meetings and contribute to some conversations that happen around the products the company offers.

3.9 Development Processes

Several years ago, a group of developers got together at Snowbird in Utah and signed what is now known as the Agile Manifesto. Since then, dozens of "agile methodologies" have popped up providing processes for building software.

If you haven't worked under a number of different systems for getting work done, you may not be able to differentiate between the methodologies in a nuanced way, but you can make some decisions about how often you check code in, how work is assigned, and how you're expected to participate in the process.

It also turns out that participating in the processes is a great way to learn how to successfully build software.

Box 3.3. Chaos preferred?

My least favorite freelance client was one where I was part of a team working on healthcare software. They didn't have a strong process. The team estimated how long tasks would take, but when it came time to assign out work, people would pick up whatever they wanted and most developers on the team had their own turf staked out. So, when I'd pick up a feature to build or a bug to fix, I'd get a couple hours in and then have someone swoop in and tell me that they were already working on it.

Some people seemed to thrive under those conditions. I didn't and eventually left that gig.

3.10 Opportunities for Growth

In my interviews leading up to this book, this was the most often cited reason for people changing jobs. Many people feel like they're stifling in their job or that they're not learning skills or technologies that allow them to stay competitive in the larger software development market.

Some ways that this particular complaint surfaces is that the company refuses to pay for training, send their developers to conferences, or support open source contributions.

The other version of this is where a software developer isn't eligible to move into a more favorable position within the company. At least two of the people I talked to had been passed over for promotions within the company. Several were looking for pay raises. And, a few wanted to move from one team to another. One in particular was looking to move up from the maintenance team—where his primary responsibility was to fix bugs and do advanced level tech support—to the feature team which added new features to the technology.

3.11 How To Design Your Dream Job: Choosing Your Top 3 "Must Haves"

Now that we've looked at the different areas of a company's profile and things you should consider regarding the companies or kinds of companies you want to work for, let's design your dream job.

As we design your dream job, keep in mind that you're probably not going to find the perfect company that ticks all the boxes. However, most developers are looking for a company that hits 2 or 3 big things.

You may care more about the corporate mission than you do about having the highest salary. You may need more time off and better health benefits. You may need to feel like you're making a difference for your co-workers, getting paid what you're worth, and have opportunities to contribute to open source.

Whatever makes you tick, narrow it down to 2 or 3 things you must have. You can have a list of 4 through 6 that'll help you decide on competing offers, but having those 2 or 3 will help you quickly identify companies that you want to target in your job search. We'll show you how to use your "Top 3" in the next chapter.

Chapter 4: Researching Companies

When researching companies, you're looking for 2 types of things. The first type is anything that relates to your Top 3. The second type is information about what they're looking for that you can use to enhance your resume and put into your cover letter.

4.1 Finding Companies that Match Your Top 3

Now that we know what your top 3 are, let's dive into finding out if a company lines up with what you want. For the more concrete things like salary, benefits, company size, etc. the information is relatively easy to find. For the softer aspects of work like the company's culture, mission, etc. you'll have to do a bit of interpretation based on what the company publishes about itself. And, finally, for things involving the day-to-day, you can get some information from the website, but the most helpful information on this particular track will come from talking to employees.

4.1.1 Where to Start

The best place to get information on a company is by talking to their employees. If you know one, take him or her to lunch. If not, then here's a breakdown of how to find information online and how to find employees to get better information from.

If your Top 3 includes location, then go to LinkedIn.com and find companies near you. You can do this by clicking the "Search" at the top and selecting "Jobs." Hit "All Filters" and enter where you live in the field under "Location." Then check the box for "Computer Software" under "Industry." Then click "Apply."

Now you have a list of companies that are in your area that are hiring.

You can get another list of companies by doing a "People" search and setting the "Locations" dropdown to include the city or area you live in.

You can add an additional filter for the "Computer Software" industry.

These will be the companies you want to look into first.

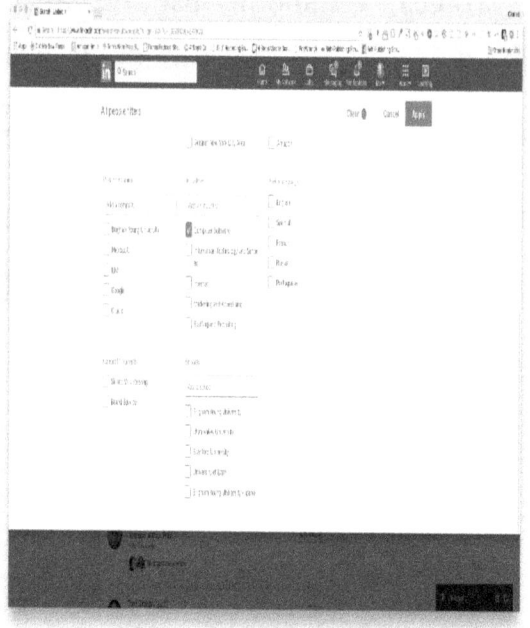

For those looking for remote jobs, put the word "remote" in the "Title" field to see if you come back with any remote software developers in your area.

If your Top 3 includes salary, benefits, or working conditions, your best bet is to start with Glassdoor.com then the company's website. If none of these made your Top 3, we'll show you how to dive into the company's website. After those resources, we'll move on to LinkedIn.

4.2 GlassDoor.com

GlassDoor.com is a terrific resource for getting information about companies. A lot of the information is provided by current and past employees of the company. All the information they enter is gathered anonymously and aggregated to give you a picture of what it's like being at that company.

This means that the salaries, benefits, and reviews posted are generally accurate since there's almost no chance that the company will be able to narrow down the person who posted the reviews and salaries unless their review contains some information that identifies them.

For our examples, I'm going to use a company near me that several of my friends have worked at over the last few years. That company is Instructure.

You can see that they have information on job openings, salaries, interviews, benefits, and reviews of the company.

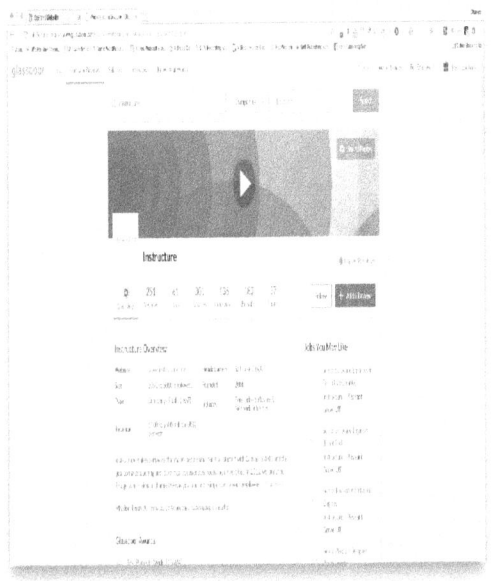

Let's start by looking at the salaries. You can see on the page, that Software Engineers at Instructure make $91.4k per year. If you're new, you'll note that the lower salaries land around $65. and the higher ones hit around $130k. You can drill in further by clicking the job title "Software Engineer."

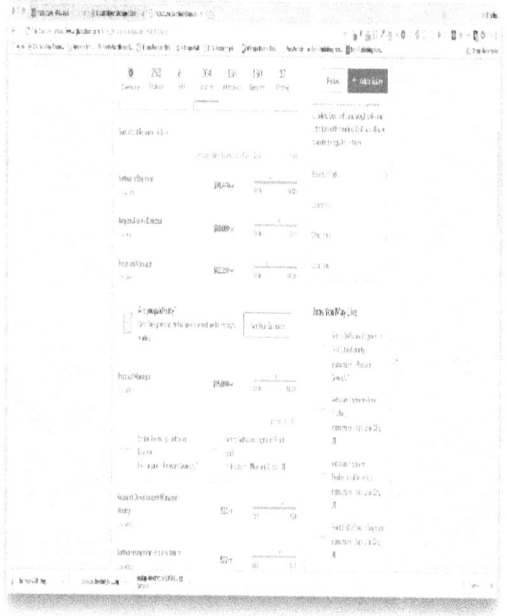

If benefits are more your thing, you can click on that tab as well. The thing that's nice about this particular view on GlassDoor.com is that you not only get the benefits that the company lists, but employee reviews of the benefits as well.

In this particular instance, you can see what they offer as well as one review that says that they offer a lower 401k match due to their offering of stock options. Whatever the case, it's usually a good idea to look over the reviews to see how they line up with what the company says it offers. I generally tell you to look at the 5 star and 1 star reviews to see what people complained about and what people raved about.

Keep in mind that the 1-star reviews sometimes come from disgruntled people, but it does give you something to ask about as you dive in and talk to employees from the company. You may mention the review on GlassDoor only to get a response like "Yeah, we had some issues with our health insurance provider, but we switched last year and things are much better now."

For other items that made your Top 3, look at the About section on the company's Glassdoor page as well as the reviews from former employees.

4.2.1 Resume and Cover Letter Materials

The most valuable part of GlassDoor, once you've decided to apply to a company, is the interviews section. This section has information from people who have interviewed at the company and often details what questions they ask.

The reason this is helpful over the Jobs section is that Job listings are horrible for giving you the information you need. The interviews are designed to figure out if you're the kind of person they want to hire. If you can glean that information and put it into your resume, you'll easily stand out.

Here's a review from someone who actually accepted an offer at Instructure...

Besides being able to see how the interview is structured, you have this statement at the end of the *Interview Questions* section: "The coding problems did not focus on algorithm. They focused on how to solve problems and OO Design."

What this tells you is that if you can put some OO (Object Oriented) design experience and problem solving experience into your resume, that will stand out. You can also add a line into your cover letter that explains that you've gotten into OO design and have been experimenting with different design patterns as ways to solve common problems. Just make sure you've begun doing this if you add them to the cover letter and resume.

Heading back to the *Jobs* section of GlassDoor.com, you'll find the job listings are pretty generic. This is because most hiring managers simply rattle off a few things they want in employees, get HR to post the listing, and hope for the best. This is why they mostly look the same.

The things you can pull from them are technologies being used, skills they're looking for, and the sort of project you'll be working on. So, if they have a long list of things they want, take it under advisement, spend a little time familiarizing yourself with the items you don't know, and then if you really want to work there, work the rest of this process to get hired there.

4.3 The Company's Website

The company's website is a sort of catch-all for information about the company. The front page is generally aimed at the company's customers and potential customers—not you. However, there is some value is knowing how they represent themselves to their customers and what their stated vision is. The way the present themselves to their customers is often a reflection of the corporate culture and communication style.

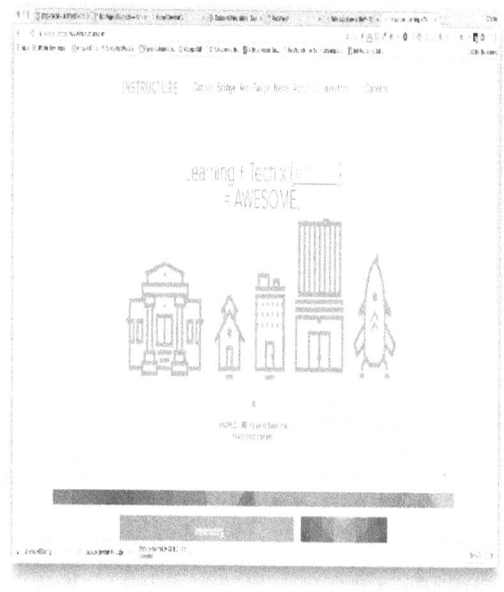

In this one, you'll see the company's mission statement "INSTRUCTURE makes software that makes people smarter" which is cited in other places on their website.

The pages you're most interested in are the About page and the Hiring or Jobs or Careers page.

4.3.1 The About Page

The company's about page will generally give you a lot of information about where they're located, how they were founded, and what they would like to achieve as a company. This last item is particularly interesting if the company's mission or making a difference made it into your Top 3.

I've also seen employee profiles of key players within the company show up on an About Page. On Instructure's page, you can see their story,

their key players,

and their corporate values. (*OK, so I found the corporate values on the Careers page...*) One caution on corporate values: for come companies, those values are what drive everything and for others, they're a trendy way to make investors feel good. The only way to know for certain which one is which is to spend some time with one of their employees and ask them what their corporate values are. If the employee doesn't know them, then the corporation isn't steered by them.

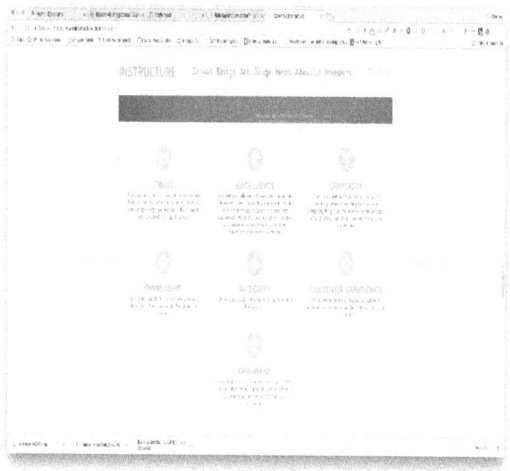

Keep in mind that if the company does care about their listed values, make sure to sprinkle those words into your cover letter and resume.

4.3.2 The Careers Page

The Careers or Hiring page is usually different from company to company. And, instead of catering to customers, they're catering to you. Most careers pages include a link to a list of their open positions. Instructure's includes a button that says "JOIN US" that links to their open positions. Instead, they've chosen to tell you what they want you to know.

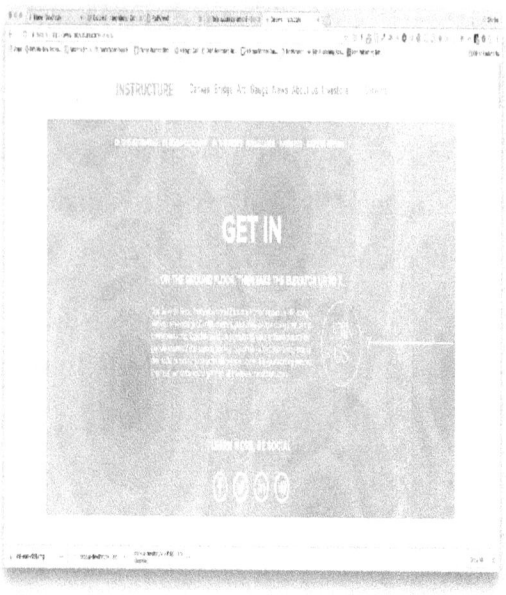

Really good careers pages will also give you some idea of who works at a company, what it's like to work there, what the office is like, and the perks they offer. In Instructure's case, they've put videos up that highlight those things for you to watch and make a decision on.

You can also see that they've listed their perks and benefits.

4.4 Social Media, Blogs, and YouTube

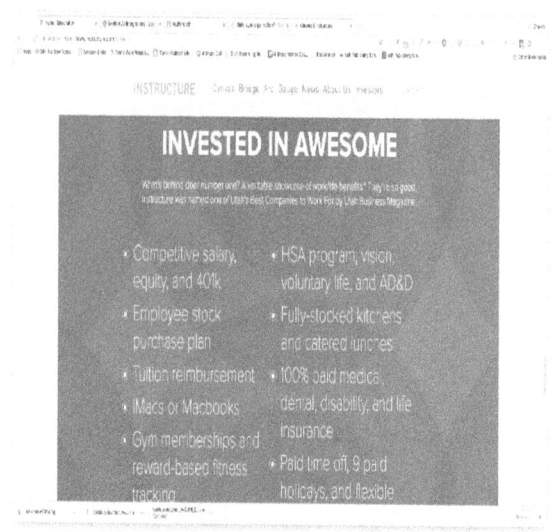

For our purposes, we've lumped social media, blog posts, and youtube into one group. The reason for this is that they all fall under forms of corporate outreach and image. In a lot of ways, the information the company puts on GlassDoor.com is also corporate outreach and image, but in that particular case, that information is aimed at job seekers rather than at the public or potential customers.

The things companies say about themselves can be important and often reflects the company's internal structure, their culture, and mission. You'll also see what they share that other people are saying about them.

Youtube also typically includes talks at corporate events and videos made by the company to sell product or get attention.

Some of this will be valuable to you, but only to the extent that you care about what people are saying about the company and what the company says about itself.

4.5 Employees

The most valuable place to get information about a company is their employees. This is the reason that Glassdoor.com is so helpful. Most of their information comes directly from former and current employees.

This is also why I recommend that you start out looking at Glassdoor.com and Linkedin.com. On Glassdoor, you can gather enough information to know what to ask about and what things they have that will or won't work for you. LinkedIn provides you with a way to find out about individual employees and to connect with them.

In Section sec:linkedin research about LinkedIn, we'll go over how to find people in LinkedIn and how to connect with them. Once you're in contact with them, there are a couple of ways you can connect with them and a few things you should definitely ask about.

4.5.1 Connecting with Employees

If it's possible, you should connect with them in person. If you can't, then find a way to connect with them online and figure out a way to make it pay off for them. One easy way to do this is to see if they'd like to meet up with you for lunch. Lunch is a nice gesture and you can pay for two lunches at a mid range restaurant for $20-$30 in the U.S. The information you get will be worth much more than that.

If you can't meet in person for lunch, ask them if they'd be willing to talk to you on a video call using Google Hangouts, Skype, or something similar. If you can schedule the call a few days out, find out what their favorite brand of coffee or soda is and order some to be delivered to their desk. If you can get it to them the day before the call, that would be ideal. They'll probably happily give you more than the 5-10 minutes you asked for.

If all you can get is a phone call, take it. But as close to face-to-face as you can get will make a huge difference. Also, remember to send them that treat if you're not meeting for lunch.

4.5.2 What to Ask

Salary is almost always in my students' Top 3. It's also generally a taboo subject and may even be considered a trade secret within the company—in other words, they're not likely to tell you what they make. So, instead of asking "How much do you make?" or "How much are developers paid at your company?" you can ask "How much do you think I'd make if I got hired at a company like <Insert name of company here>?"

The reason this is non-threatening is because you're asking in general, even though they're likely to answer you specifically with the company they work at in mind. If they ask if you want to know what their company will pay you, just say "Yes, but I don't want you to share anything that's proprietary with your employer. So, if it won't get you in trouble, then yes."

For health benefits, usually if this made your Top 3, you're worried about keeping your doctor, covering an ongoing medical condition, or are at risk for one thing or another. If this fits your bill, the best thing to find out is which insurance company they get coverage from and if possible what plans they offer. If they have their insurance card on them—most people carry a copy with them—you can look up the plan to see what they cover and look on their website to see if your doctor is listed.

Even if it's not in your top 3, it's also worthwhile to find out what hours they usually work, what the time expectations are, what the corporate dress code is, and what sort of machine they use.

You'll also want to find out how the team they work on operates. Do people tend to work in the same silos? or do they spread the work around among the team? Are there multiple products? Are there cross-product or cross-functional teams? Do they follow some methodology for getting things done or assigning work?

Also, make sure to find out about their boss. Considering that their boss will probably end up being your boss, the more you can find out, the better you can prepare for interviews and be aware of any pitfalls or payoffs you'll gain from working with their boss.

Finally, see if you can get a tour of their office. If you can't go there in person, see if they'll give you a virtual tour with their phone or laptop.

4.6 LinkedIn

LinkedIn is easily the most valuable place for information about the company. Companies aren't necessarily better about putting information here, but their employees are. It's also a great place to find a way to network with employees from the company you want to work with.

To find people at the company you're targeting, click the Search bar and select People. Then type the name of the company in the Company dropdown.

Now that you've got a list of employees who work for the company, look through them to see if you can find any 1st degree connections. These are people you've actually connected with on LinkedIn. If you haven't used LinkedIn before, that's

OK, you simply won't have any 1st or 2nd degree connections. In fact, you may want to import contacts from your email account so that you will know who you can connect through to get introduced to people. Even if you don't do this, you can

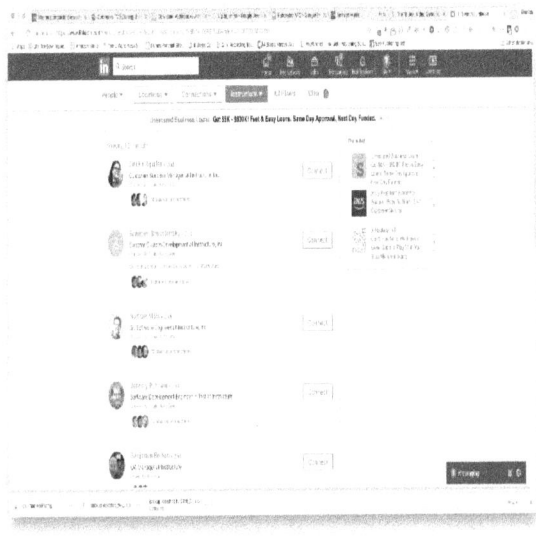

still reach out to them through LinkedIn.

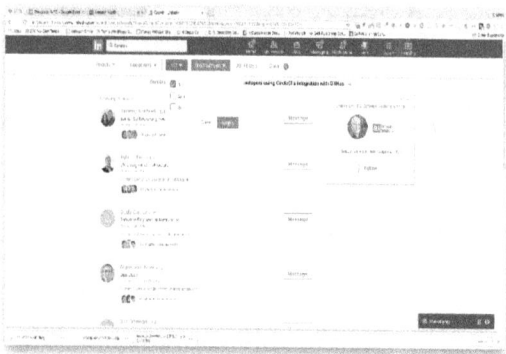

1st degree connections are people you already know. In this case, I know several people at Instructure because their current CEO is the founder of my first job out of college and he wound up hiring a bunch of people he knew from that job.

If you know that person well, just email, text or call them to see when they can get together for a meeting. If you don't know them well or don't have their contact information, you can get their email address by clicking their name and then *See contact info.*

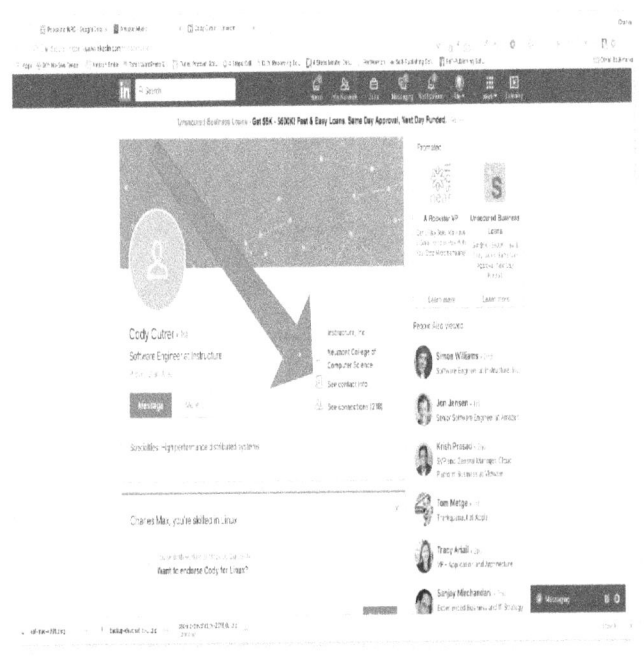

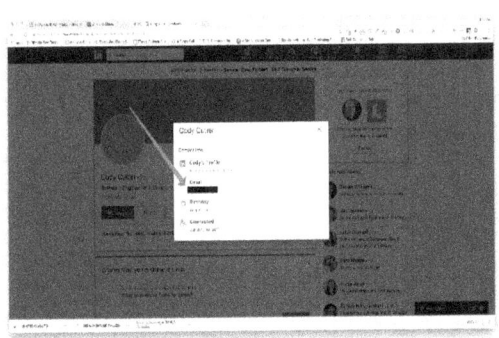

If you don't have any promising 1st

connections, you're next best bet is to add them as a connection on LinkedIn and see if you can figure out what their email is for follow up.

To add them as a connection, just click the *Connect* button in the search results you got and send them a message like this:

Hi <Name>!

My name is <Name>. I recently graduated from <Bootcamp> and I'm interested in working at <Company>. Before I apply, I was wondering if I can buy you lunch and pick your brain about what it's like working there. I'm trying to get a good read on what types of developers you hire over there, what management is like, and how you work.

Thanks, <Name>

If you don't hear back in a couple of days, then send an email mentioning that you tried to reach out on LinkedIn. To avoid the creepy factor of you getting their email address from nowhere, tell them you made an educated guess based on their name and the company's domain.

Box 4.1. Finding Email Addresses Outside of LinkedIn You can find the email addresses of people you are connected to on LinkedIn. But, what if you send a message to someone LinkedIn and they don't log in enough to see it? This is where I recommend another service called <u>Hunter.io</u>.

You can get a free account where you can do 25 or so lookups per month. That's plenty for most of the prospecting you'll be doing.

Once you're in Hunter, enter the company your prospective contact works for.

Enter the name of the person you're looking for.

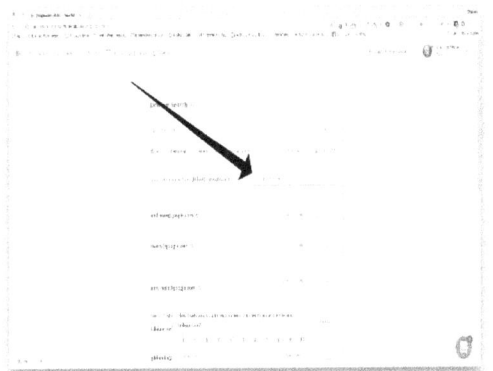 If Hunter.io can find their email address somewhere on the internet, it'll show it to you.

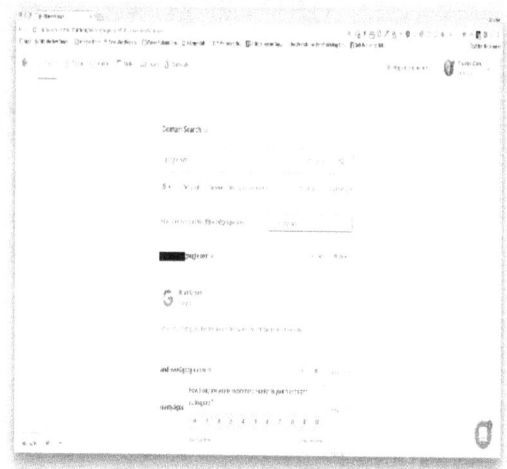

If it can't, then it'll give you its best guess and a common pattern for finding other email addresses.

This is your "educated guess based on their name and the company they work for" if they ask how you got their email address.

Besides giving you ways of reaching employees of the companies you're pursuing, LinkedIn also provides a ton of information about the companies themselves.

Most of the information you'll find on LinkedIn is also available on social media or on Glassdoor.com. However, there are a few things you can find on the LinkedIn page that are extremely useful.

Because I have a premium LinkedIn account, I get a few views into LinkedIn data that free users won't. Find someone who can look this up if you can. If you can't, then do your best without it.

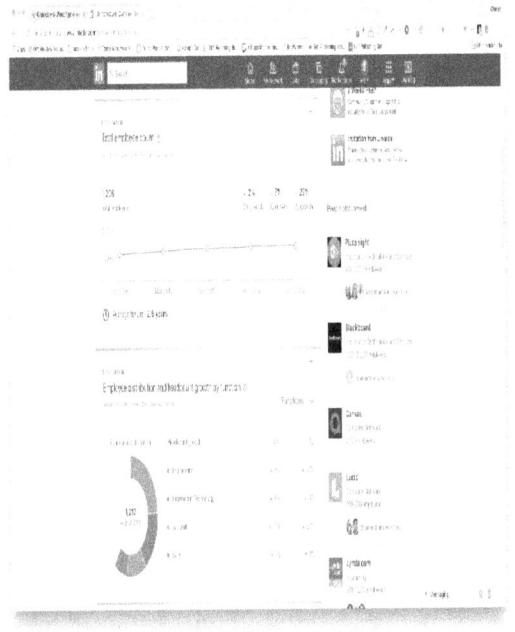

From the linked in hiring stats, you can see if the company is growing. If they are, it's generally a good sign that they are either making money or getting investment. In this example,]you can also see that 29% of their growth over the last year has been in Engineering and IT. That's also a good sign that they're expanding offerings, taking on new projects, and very likely adopting new technologies or at least working with the latest versions of their current technology stacks.

Finally, you can see if they've increased their headcount. In this example, it's clear that they've increased their

Engineering hiring by more than 10x. If they're hiring that many more developers, then you have a decent shot of getting hired if you look like someone they can onboard quickly.

Chapter 5: Resumes that Work

Your resume has one job: getting you an interview. In this chapter, we're going to show you how to put together a resume that will give you the best chance of getting an interview.

Keep in mind that Chapter 4 about corporate research is going to play a major role here. If you know what the company is looking for and what it's like to work there you can tailor your resume to best represent how you'll fit in and contribute once you're hired.

You will also want to make sure that you've gone over Chapter 6 to learn how to write a compelling cover letter to accompany your resume.

5.1 Formatting Your Resume

Most employers and HR departments don't really read resumes. They scan them for the information they want. So, the key to formatting your resume is making information easy to find and making your resume easy to skim.

The most important information should be closest to the top. So, if the company puts a lot of stock in having a college degree, your education should be at the top. If they care more about open source contributions than job experience—most won't—then put your resume in that order.

If you don't have any relevant job experience, then you'll prioritize your open source contributions, blog posts, podcasts, videos, and/or side projects to demonstrate your ability to code.

Generally, your resume will follow this ordering from top to bottom unless you learn something about the employer that makes you move something up.

1. Your Name
2. Contact Information—phone number and email address
3. Education
4. Job Experience
5. Open Source contributions
6. Side Projects
7. Media—blogs, podcasts, videos, etc.
8. Other social and volunteer activities that are relevant to what they do

A quick rundown of why we chose this order is as follows. We start with your name so that they know whose resume they are looking at and who they're calling to set up an interview.

We place contact information next since the outcome we're aiming for is getting a phone call for an interview.

Education comes next, mostly because it's easy to skim by and pick up any information they care about before they get to what really matters to them—job experience. We follow it up with open source contributions since they can bring some prestige and will demonstrate that you can work well with others.

Then side projects that demonstrate what you can do and any media work since it allows them to sample what you know.

Social and volunteer activities can give them some idea of who you are and what you care about as well as give you a cancel to call out anything you have in common with other employees or managers you're considering working with.

Box 5.1. Resume Tip: Placing Your Contact Information in the Right Margin When I was a freshman in college, we were assigned a resume to write for our English class. Our professor showed us a trick where if we put our contact information in the right hand margin of the resume. The reason being that when the resume was turned on its side and placed in a folder by a right-handed person, that contact information would appear at the top of the page.

He also told us to right-justify our names at the top of the resume so it would also appear whenever someone was thumbing through the stack of resumes.

This puts your contact information front and center the next time Human

Resources or a man ager thumbs through the pile looking for likely candidates.

Here's an image of what it looks like. Give it a try! Grab this book with your right hand and turn it on its side. How does this resume format work for you?

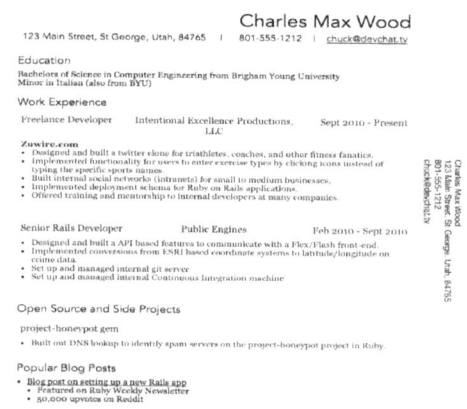

Yes, this only really works for resumes that get printed, but it does make your contact information stand out anyway.

Your name should be at the very top of your resume. You want the reader to associate everything they're gathering from the resume with your name.

Right below this should be your contact information. At a minimum, it should include your phone number—preferably a cell phone number—and email address. Some people also list their website. Don't add anything else unless they ask for it. Social media links and other information are generally not useful and can distract from what you really want them to know about you.

Once you've got your contact information included, show off your education. If that's bootcamp or a college degree, list it. If you have a college degree in something that is not technical, list that here too. It shows that your teachable and gives them an idea of what you're good at.

Bootcamps and technical degrees demonstrate training and aptitude in technical areas.

Next comes job experience. If this is your first programming job, list any technology related work experience first. If you don't have any relevant job experience at all, then list your side projects and media presence that shows off your programming skills first and your non-technical job experience further down in your resume.

What they encounter first is what makes the biggest impression. So, you want them to encounter your capabilities in the area of programming before they encounter your lack of on-the-job experience. They'll begin to justify your lack of experience in their head with what they've seen that you're capable of doing.

When you list out your previous jobs and side projects, use bullet points to highlight each thing that you've done on those projects. Your bullet points should be informed by your research into the company and what technologies they use and technical challenges they need solved.

Box 5.2. Public Engines: How I Got Hired for Knowing What They Needed

In 2010, my friend mentioned that the company he was working for was hiring. I wasn't happy in the job I was at, so I asked him if I could apply. He took my resume in and I got called in by his boss, Karl, for an interview.

At the time, I only had 2 years experience as a full time developer and Karl let me know that he was looking for someone with more experience than what I had. However, as we talked, it became apparent that I had some skills that they needed—I had set up continuous integration with Jenkins at my previous job and had handled a good deal of the devops needs for my team.

The company had an ops team that managed the servers, but they were too busy to help the development team with all of their infrastructure needs. The fact was that my friend, David, had clued me in that they needed this type of work done and that was the reason he had recommended that I apply.

So, I had picked up the resume I had been sending to other companies, and added those things to it and moved them into a position where they'd be noticed. Then I made sure to bring them up in the interview.

When I got hired, Karl reiterated that he was worried was still "too green" but that he needed my experience in providing infrastructure and that David had vouched for my development skills.

Not only did I get hired, but I got the salary I had asked for.

When most people build their resumes, they list the most recent project or job first. Your most recent job experience is also usually the most relevant and most employers expect this. However, if you have less recent but more relevant job experience, list it first. Then put everything else in chronological order.

On each job listing, put each accomplishment in its own bullet point on its own line. Keep the number of bullet points to no more than 5 or 6 unless all of them address specific needs of the job you're applying to.

Start each bullet point with an action word. Avoid generic statements as well. Use a thesaurus if you need to.

For example, "Built in authentication with devise Ruby gem" isn't as impressive as "Customized authentication using devise to allow multiple email addresses to be used at login." The reason is that anyone who has used the devise gem knows that it's used to set up authentication and that it's not that difficult. The word "built" will also describe most of the coding work you do, so find better words. By saying that you customized the devise gem, you're demonstrating that your knowledge goes well beyond the normal usage of the library and gives you the air of a more senior developer. Being specific shows a certain level of skill as well.

5.2 Example Resume

Here's an example resume I put together that I'll walk you through to give you some concrete ideas on how yours can work.

5.2.1 Formatting

One thing you'll note is that I don't have

any lines across it at all or any fancy formatting beyond just basic layout. For some people, the horizontal lines under the section titles help them skip to the relevant sections, for others they don't. My personal taste is to leave them off, but you can add them in if you'd like.

You'll also see that I like to space things out a bit. I use tables for the horizontal spacing since both Microsoft Word and Pages on the Mac will automatically space table cells out evenly. Then I can left justify the left cell, right justify the right cell, and center the middle cell to give it an even, easy to scan feel.

Use sans-serif fonts for your names, contact information, and header. Use serif fonts for everything else.

5.2.2 Contact Information

As mentioned before, put your contact information at the top and in the right margin. For the contact information in the right margin create a text-box and rotate it to get it where you want it. Right justify your name to make it the first thing the reader sees when they pull it out of a pile with their right hand.

5.2.3 Education

Place the Education section next because it's short and easy to skim past if the employer doesn't care. You'll also notice that I didn't list a GPA and that I did list a non-technical minor.

You shouldn't list your GPA unless it will impress the reader. So, if you had a 4.0, list it. A 3.3 or 3.4 grade point average is about as low as I'd go before just leaving it off. 3.0 is basically an average student who didn't have too many poor grades. My GPA was 2.97, which, even though it's just shy of 3.0, is low enough to turn a few folks off because it's not 3.0.

I left the Italian minor on because to demonstrates that I have skills beyond coding. If you have a non-technical degree, it's still worth listing because it shows that you're willing to work to gain knowledge and skills. I also confess that I lived in Italy for 2 years and tested out of 90% of the courses required for that minor, but the company I'm applying to doesn't need to know that. If they ask, I can talk about living in Italy for 2 years and gain points for having life experience.

5.2.4 Freelancing

You'll notice that the first section in my job experience is my Freelance experience. I listed it like another job, but you can add it with its own header and then list contract jobs like regular jobs. As a freelancer over 6 years, I probably worked a dozen or so contracts, so it'd turn into a long list. If this is your experience, then list the most relevant or impressive ones and put a note in your resume that says "Full freelancing history available upon request." This lets them know that you've done other work that isn't in the resume.

You can also see that I limited myself to 5 bullet points on the contract. Obviously, if you did most of the work on that project, you could list many more things you contributed to that project.

You shouldn't because it's not all relevant and if they want to know more, they'll invite you in for an interview and you can discuss that work experience with them then.

5.2.5 Work Experience

In each job listing, the things that stand out are the position title, company, and dates you worked there. Some companies put a lot of stock into how long or how continuously you were employed. So, be prepared to explain any gaps in the interview. The only answer to this that might cause you trouble is if you have a gap where you were looking for a job and couldn't find one. And, even then, if you can explain that you updated your resume to give employers a better idea of what you can do, they'll probably accept it. The only explanation that hurts you is that you couldn't get a job because of some character flaw that other interviewers saw in you.

The job listing then has the bullet points as mentioned before. Start with 4 in here that demonstrate specific skills you think employers might want and then swap them out if you find out that there was something else that the employer was interested in.

You'll notice that the last two were setting up internal tools for the project. You can list things like that because those are things that not many other developers have done. That helps you stand out and lets them know that you can solve unique team wide problems even if your experience isn't a direct match with what they think they're looking for.

5.2.6 Open Source and Side Projects

This section is there primarily to let your prospective employer know that you're consistently contributing to the community at large and to give them some idea of what you work on in your free time. It also tells them that you are passionate about writing code and in particular what areas of code you'll write even if you're not getting paid.

They can also go check those out to get an idea of your personal coding style and what tools and techniques you use to write your software.

If you have a commit bit to any open source projects that are widely used, you should mention that here. Many open source software maintainers take contributions to their projects from the community. If you consistently make high quality contributions, the maintainers will sometimes allow you to make contributions without review. Programmers call this a "commit bit." Otherwise, you'll likely be making your submissions through "Pull Requests" which have to be merged into a project by a committer—someone with a commit bit.

For side projects, make sure you have a well written README file that explains what the project is and how to set it up.

5.2.7 Blog Posts, Podcasts, and Screencasts

You can see that the last section is Blog Posts. If you're extremely prolific blogger, podcaster, or screencaster, then it may make sense to put this ahead of your job experience. This is actually the case for me. I've been podcasting for over 10 years and have recorded at least 1,000 podcast episodes. If you're just getting started, leave it where it is and see if you can get a blog post or YouTube video to get some attention.

With this section, you're hoping to provide some social proof. Social proof is essentially public information that demonstrates that other people buy into what you're doing. So, if you have a blog post that's been viewed thousands of times, been featured in a newsletter, or gotten a bunch of tweets or retweets, it shows that you understand things on a level that allows you to easily share it with other people.

Box 5.3. Promoting Blog Posts and Other Content

Getting visitors to your website and reading your articles is actually not terribly hard. And, if you can get thousands of visits or reads, you can put it on your resume as proof that you stand out.

There are 3 places you'll want to go to promote your content: email newsletters, link sharing websites, and other content producers.

For newsletters, all you need to do is go to the newsletter's website and find out how to submit an article. It's typically done by email or a web form. If you get rejected, ask them what topics or content they're looking for and then write that article next. It may also pay to go read a few back issues of the newsletter to see what they're publishing and what the articles are saying about their topics.

My favorite newsletters are published by Cooper Press.

On link sharing websites, the process has 2 steps. First, submit the article to the website. Then, go ask your friends to comment on it or upvote it. Two popular websites to submit to about software development are Reddit and DZone. There are also a few that are focused on particular languages and topics like JavaScript.com and RubyFlow.

When you approach other content producers, generally you want to offer to do something for them, then ask them to mention your article in one of theirs. You'll also want to make sure that the article you're promoting is high enough quality for them to endorse it. If you can get good traction from the other two promotion methods mentioned in this aside, then it's probably good enough.

For example, if I got an email from someone saying "I tweeted about the last 3 episodes of Ruby Rogues. I'd also like to share this testimonial for Get a Coder Job." I'd be delighted. Then if you mentioned that you wrote an article based on something out of Ruby Rogues (or one of the other Devchat.tv podcasts) I'd likely share it if I thought my audience would enjoy it and it's high quality.

Not all content providers will do this and people get busy, so you may need to follow up.

Finally, make sure that you don't submit resumes without doing research and presenting a cover letter. If you can have an employee at the company submit your resume for you or if you can hand it in in person, that's typically ideal. We'll talk in future chapters about how to get that done.

Chapter 6: Cover Letters

Cover Letters are an essential part of your resume. Your resume's job is to convey to your potential employer what kinds of things you can do for them. Your cover letter fills in the gaps in your resume that you can't convey well in your resume by telling them what kind of person you are, what kind of employee you'll be, and why you're applying to work with them.

Imagine for a second that you're the employer. You have two resumes. One demonstrates that the person has nearly all the job skills you want. The other person has included a cover letter that shows you that they're committed to learning, they work well with other people, and they've adequately explained that what your company does is very much inline with how they see themselves and the difference they want to make in the world.

Nearly every hiring manager I've talked to would take the second candidate in two heartbeats. The reason is that they know that this person will be a pleasure to work with and will be committed to the company's mission. They'll give far more than the first candidate. Plus, as long as they can contribute in meaningful ways, they can be trained to have the other skills that the employer will need them to have to make them the ideal employee.

The prevailing wisdom is generally not to include a cover letter. The reasoning being that many employers don't look at them and that it's extra work for everyone involved.

Even if this is true, there will be some employers that will read it. Giving them more reasons and more personal reasons to hire you is never a bad thing. Plus, many applicants who send in cover letters provide generic information in the cover letter instead of doing the research to know what the cover letter needs to include in the first place.

Because you're doing the work to research the company and figure out what the company and potential boss needs, the cover letter will clearly express why you're the ideal candidate for the job.

With the information we've gathered thus far on the companies you want to work for, you'll find that it's pretty easy to write a cover letter. You can quickly and easily connect the dots on how you'll fit in at the company and the reasons you have for going out of your way to apply there.

6.1 The Four Parts of a Cover Letter

A cover letter has four main parts: the introduction, why you want to work for the company, showing that you're the kind of person they're looking for, and an invitation to contact you. There are some other things that people generally add to cover letters like contact information and the general letter formatting like the salutation and signature.

Here's an example of a cover letter if I were applying to jobs today.

Box 6.1. Example Cover Letter

Charles Max Wood

123 Main Street

St. George, Utah, 84654

(801)555-1212
chuck@devchat.tv
Bob,

Over the last 12 years of full time software development experience, I've had the opportunity to build and architect multiple complex systems like social networks and blogging platforms. I've also produced over 1,000 podcast episodes in which I've taught, learned, and discussed concepts around Ruby, JavaScript, React, Vue, Angular, Elixir, and many other programming languages and frameworks as well as freelancing.

As I've looked into Instructure, I noticed that you are committed to providing a solution that helps people get smarter. I'm committed to helping the world be a better place and believe that by giving educators—of which I consider myself one—the tools to guide people to learn the skills they need to succeed in the world we can change the world.

I've also talked to some of your employees and found that you hire extremely qualified and talented people. I look forward to the opportunity to work with them. I feel that within this elite crowd, I bring some unique perspectives having built SaaS applications for my own needs and having architected and built specific systems for various clients, along with my work as a full time employee working on crime and location data, building automation systems to increase team efficiency, and applying general DevOps solutions.

I also love learning and have spoken many times at conferences and local user's groups alongside the podcasts and video work I've done in the past.

Feel free to look over my resume and reach out if you have any questions. I believe you'll find that I have the skills to contribute to and lead any team I join and will help them make greater contributions to the company and the world at large.

Thank you for your consideration,

Charles Max Wood

Now that we have an example to work from, let's break this cover letter down and look at each of the 4 parts.

6.1.1 The Introduction

The introduction in the cover letter is basically a summary of your resume. It introduces the employer to you, but it also highlights the parts of your resume you want them to pay particular attention to. While you don't explicitly call this out, if they read the cover letter first, their minds will naturally gravitate to those parts of the resume.

It also gives some context for the rest of the cover letter by providing them with a description of what you believe your qualifications are.

A good introduction will do the following:

- List your achievements.
- Highlight any relevant skills or knowledge you have.
- Let them know how long you've been working in the field.
- Note any other qualifications you have.

In our example, you can see that it lists my achievements. It talks about building and architecting social networks and recording over 1,000 podcasts. If you're new, these could be graduating from a bootcamp, building particular side projects, participating in open source projects, writing a blog, and many other things. If you're an experienced developer, this will likely be more on the side of how you've taken leadership on a team, specific contributions to projects at the jobs you've held, and any areas you're especially skilled in or in which you've pioneered unique solutions.

Your introduction should be no more than 1 paragraph long. Anything essential that would make it longer than a paragraph should be worked into the other parts of the cover letter. For example, you'll notice that I worked the bit about freelancing and the bit about podcasts into other parts of the resume. That gave it emphasis. However, if I were applying to a company where I had direct experience and couldn't fit it all into the introduction. I'd mention it while talking about why I'd like to work for them by stating that "I especially enjoyed…" doing the thing they do "while working on…" that other project that looks a lot like theirs.

6.1.2 Tell Them Why You Want to Work There

Once you're done introducing yourself, you'll tell them why you want to work for them. Generally, this will involve your top 3. You'll also want to show the company that you've done a bit of research into them. Since most job candidates don't put forward that much effort it'll make you stand out.

In particular, this section demonstrates that you know enough about the company to know that you'll be a good fit for them and them for you. Turnover is expensive. It costs a company money to train new employees and they have lower productivity levels when someone is coming up to speed. So, having someone who will be happy working for them and will stay for a long time is highly beneficial to the company.

If you've ever worked with one, you'll know that working with someone who is a jerk or who is unhappy with the job and/or employer, you'll realize that's a big drag on a team as well and may cause other employees to leave.

So, demonstrating fit and telling them why you'll be happy at their company is a good way to alleviate some of their worries about hiring you.

One way to approach this is to state your Top 3.

When I started looking for this job, I knew I wanted a place where I could have an impact on the company, help them make a difference in the world, and that had good health benefits.

Then let them know how you figured out that they were a good fit.

I spent a lot of time reading your website, talking to your employees, and browsing sites like LinkedIn.com and GlassDoor.com.

Finally, tell them what you learned. Your employees John Doe and David Smith told me that you're absolutely serious about changing the world. I've also heard about several initiatives at Instructure that I excel at and feel like I can make a real contribution. And, your health insurance package looks like it's exactly what I need.

The version in my cover letter is less explicit. I just listed what I like about the company and let the reader infer that those are things that are important to me.

Either approach will work. Just make sure it comes across that you did your research and found things you really care about in the material you went through.

6.1.3 Explain Why You're a Great Candidate

It's a fairly natural progression to move from introduction to stating a problem and then proposing a solution. The problem you stated is that the company needs someone and needs that someone to line up with their values and provide what they need. Now, you propose your solution: hiring you.

Make sure to address any areas that are core to the company, their values, and who they are. In my research into Instructure, I've found that their hiring process is fairly involved. From talking to some of my friends who have worked at Instructure, I also know that they like to hire top talent.

I focused on that aspect of why I'm a great fit because I'm going into a job interview where that will be a primary focus. The second point for why I'm a great fit went into my next paragraph. I aligned that one with their corporate mission.

> I've also talked to some of your employees and found that you hire extremely qualified and talented

people. I look forward to the opportunity to work with them. I feel that within this elite crowd, I bring some unique perspectives having built SaaS applications for my own needs and having architected and built specific systems for various clients, along with my work as a full time employee working on crime and location data, building automation systems to increase team efficiency, and applying general DevOps solutions.

I also love learning and have spoken many times at conferences and local user's groups alongside the podcasts and video work I've done in the past.

What you're hoping for here is that you've talked about yourself the same way they talk about the person they want to hire.

6.1.4 Invitation to Contact You

There are two things you need to do when you invite someone to contact you. First, you need to refer to your resume. It's pretty obvious, since you sent the cover letter with the resume, but you expect that they'll look over your resume.

The resume will back up any claims you make in the cover letter and will hopefully demonstrate to them that you have done many things that they'll want you to do for them.

Then actually invite them to contact you. Don't bother entering your email address or phone number here. That should be at the top of the page.

6.2 Other Cover Letter Guidelines

You'll notice in my example letter that I start out with my name, address, phone number, and email address. Traditionally, cover letters are formatted like letters. So the contact information goes at the top of the page. In our case, we want them to contact us, so there's no reason to change that format. You can see that the rest is formatted as a letter.

Make sure that you add extra space between paragraphs, the salutation, and the signature for easier reading and scanning. The cover letter will get skimmed as well. That's OK, people can pick up a lot of information from a quick once over on your cover letter.

As for content, you want your cover letter to resonate as much as possible with how the hiring manager and company think about themselves and their employees. So, once you've written a rough draft of your cover letter and resume, go back to the company's website and see if there are specific words and phrases used that you can bring back and incorporate into your cover letter.

One example from our sample cover letter is where I use the terms "helps people get smarter." I may want to change that to "makes people smarter" since that's what Instructure has stated is their mission.

Of course, sending in a cover letter and resume isn't a guarantee that your resume will get read. Keep in mind that the people hiring are busy doing the rest of their job. In the next chapter, we'll discuss follow up and how to stay top of mind until they get around to hiring you.

Chapter 7: Following Up

In running my own company, producing podcasts, finding freelance clients, or getting hired at a new job, the most effective way I've found to get people to do what I want them to is to follow up. Following up isn't being forceful or manipulative. Instead, it's giving the person an opportunity to do what it is that they should probably do anyway.

Remember in Chapter 2 when we talked about the overworked hiring manager trying to sort through that big pile of resumes? The reality is that he or she knows that they need to reach out to someone and get them working on their team. So, by following up, you're not being obnoxious, you're making it easy for them to hit the reply button and bring you in for an interview, which is what they should be doing anyway

When I initially wrote this chapter, I recommended that if you hadn't heard from or reached out to a company in about a week, send some form of follow up.

The reality is that the turnaround on weekly follow up is way too slow.

I'm not advocating that you send an email every day. Every 3 days is usually enough. The real trick is popping up on their radar the other 2 days between follow ups so that they'll see your name over and over again.

The method I'm going to provide you for follow up works for me finding 5 figure sponsorships for my podcasts and has worked for many of my students that I've coached through finding a job.

You should do follow up after each stage of the job hunt: applying for the job, getting interviewed, getting an offer letter and countering. The reason being that at each of these stages, someone is prone to getting busy and letting things slide. It's up to you to remind them that they need to respond to you.

Typically all you have to do is reach out. You don't even need to ask for the response, though that is a helpful step to take a lot of the time. Especially if you're past the interview stage.

7.1 Email #1

You'll want to lead out with an email. It's by far the easiest way for someone to be able to respond with a job interview invitation or job offer depending on what you're following up for.

I'm going to provide 2 examples of emails I'd sent out that you can modify for your own uses.

Hi John!

I've been looking at BigCo for a while as a place I'd like to work. I've spoken with Steve, who is one of your developers. We've had some long conversations about BigCo and what you're doing over there. I love the idea of working on a CRM that is used by so many people.

Steve said he'd drop my resume on your desk. It's been a few days and I figured you'd gotten busy. If you can reply and let me know that you got it, I'd feel better about things. Then I can follow up in a few days to see when we can meet for an interview.

I've recently graduated from a coding bootcamp in Salt Lake City and have grown to love coding. They taught us Ruby on Rails. I'm looking forward to learning more about Ruby and Rails in the near future. However, Steve mentioned that you also use React, so I've taken a course on Pluralsight on React and I'm building a recipe app to learn more.

I'm including my resume so you can see what other projects I've been involved in.

Thanks, Chuck

This email isn't very long, but it gets across that I'm interested in the company and gives John, the hiring manager, a chance to get back to me. It also quickly demonstrates that since I'm not an experienced developer, I'm working hard to get up to speed.

If John's busy, the easiest thing for him to do besides ignoring the email is to reply and ask me to come in on Monday for an interview.

If he ignores it, then we'll follow up in other ways and send an email in about 3 days.

Here's another email targeted at following up after an interview:

Hey John!

It was great coming in and talking to you last week. I really enjoyed seeing the office, meeting the team, and talking about what you need at BigCo.

I was hoping to hear back from you by now. I assume you had other candidates to interview and are doing the best you can to find a great candidate.

I wanted to quickly remind you about our discussion regarding setting up Continuous Integration for the team and helping manage some of the development practices and tools. I'd love to see how I can help increase the overall coding output for the team. I'm also excited by the prospect of working with and learning from members of the team.

Let me know if you have any other questions.

Talk soon! Chuck

PS - Say 'hi' to Steve and the rest of the team for me.

This email is really designed to help John remember who you are and what you offered as part of the team. It highlights some of the things you talked about and some of the things he said he was interested in from your background.

It also quickly gives him a chance to get back to you and let you know what's going on with the job. If he hasn't made a decision, this prompts him to do so. If he has, then you know whether or not to continue following up.

7.2 Following on Social Media

Most social media systems will alert you if someone new follows you. On Facebook and Twitter, this shows up in your notifications. On LinkedIn, there's a list of new connections or requested connections. If they look at these, they'll see your name come up just because you followed them, friended them, or tried connecting with them.

This is usually the step taken after sending that first email. Wait a day and then follow the person you followed up with on all the social platforms you can find them on. The reason you do this after sending that first email—unless you already did it as part of investigating the company—is that your email should have popped up in their inbox the day before and then they'll see your name on social media soon after that.

Just make sure that you're following them on social media that they're active on. For example, if they haven't tweeted in awhile, you can follow them on Twitter, but go check out their Facebook and LinkedIn profiles to see if they're more active on there.

The systems you should follow them on if you can find them are:

- Facebook
- Twitter
- LinkedIn
- Instagram

7.3 Interacting on Social Media

A day after following someone on social media, go look at their social media accounts and interact with something they've posted. This can come in a number of ways:

- Like their post
- Comment on their post
- Reply to their comment on a post
- Share or retweet their post

- Post something using the same hashtags they're using - This is especially useful on Instagram.

You can start with liking and sharing posts. It's not much effort and pops your name up. If that doesn't work to get their attention, then move on to commenting or replying.

When you comment or reply, one of the most effective ways is to ask an honest question. So, if there's some aspect of what's been posted that you don't understand, ask for clarification.

Many people also like thoughtful disagreement. Go read some articles that present a different point of view, and then reply stating that you read those articles and ask them for deeper thoughts on what they wrote to clarify what they're sharing.

The key here is having thoughtful interactions. Don't comment just to comment. "Thank you" is not what you want to send through. Do some research if you have to and then make your comment something they'll want to respond to.

If you're doing this the day after your email because you had already followed this person, then do this for two days before sending your next email.

7.4 Email #2: A Quick Note

After you've spent a couple of days responding to their social media, send another email to follow up again. Generally, you want this to be a "quick note" you're sending over because you're finding great stuff that they've shared in the past.

To send this email, go into your "Sent Mail" in whatever email system you use and hit "Reply." This will set the subject line to "re: Checking in" or whatever your subject was before. It also includes your last email. Because of the way email deliverability works, a certain percentage ends up in the black hole, This shows that you tried to reach out earlier, even if they didn't see it.

People are also more likely to open an email that starts with "re:"

Hi John!

I found your twitter account the other day and added ngrx to my recipe app I was building to explore different parts of Angular. Cool stuff! I really appreciate the way you explained how to structure reducers.

I just wanted to drop a quick note to see how the hiring was going and to see if you had any other tricks you could share regarding ngrx and Angular.

Thanks, Chuck

PS - My recipes app is at https://github.com/cmaxw/recipes

After sending this email, spend another 3-4 days interacting with their social media posts.

7.5 Email #3: Did I Miss Something?

The third email is usually the last email before you go weekly with your contact. Don't forget to post it as a reply to your other emails. It'll look something like this:

Hi John!

It's been great getting to know you a little during our interview and by watching your social media. I'll definitely continue reading what you're putting out there and incorporating it into my work.

My career coach told me that I should probably expect to hear back on interviews within a week or so and since it's been a week and I haven't heard back, I'm guessing you either got busy or found something who is even more amazing than me. ;)

I thought the interview went well and I still want to work for BigCo. I was wondering if there were things I could pick up that would make me more interesting to you and your team. I'm a self starter and am happy to do the work to learn how to learn things, so a quick list is all I'm asking for.

I'd love your thoughts and look forward to meeting up again sometime.

Thanks, Chuck

7.6 Alternative Follow Up Methods

Sometimes after all that, things don't work. Keep following up. Send out an email weekly for a few weeks, just in case. Spend a bit of time working social media. And keep researching new companies and working the process to get noticed. We cover how to get noticed in the next chapter.

You may also want to consider using some of these tactics after the initial follow up emails as well if you think they'd be effective. If you're not sure they'll work, try one or two anyway.

7.6.1 Postal Mail

Sending something in the mail is actually pretty novel. Most people just don't do that kind of thing anymore unless they work for Amazon's shipping department.

If you've done your research on a person and know what they like, you can have something they really like sent to their office. And, due to the law of reciprocity, they'll want to do something nice back. So, prompt them to give you a call.

For example, imagine the hiring manager is a huge Philadelphia Eagles fan. Of course they won the Super Bowl in 2018! All the other Eagles fans are talking about the big victory until the next Super Bowl. So, you hop on Amazon and have them wrap up a 2018 Super Bowl champions mug and ship it off to the manager with a card.

The card says:

I'd feel like a champion with a coach like you! I'd love to discuss my resume and job opportunities with you.

Give me a call at (801)555-1212.

Chuck (a.k.a. Charles Max Wood)

Yes, it's a little cheesy, but what do you think the odds are of getting a call back?! And, given the downside is not getting the job, I'd say you have nothing to lose.

I looked on Amazon.com and saw that an [Eagles coffee mug](#) costs around $20 with shipping. Would you spend $20 or so to get a chance to work at a company that matches your Top 3?

For more ideas on how to use postal mail, check out [Chapter cha:postal_mail](#) on getting noticed using postal mail.

7.6.2 Going into the Office

Going into the office is one of the strategies I put forward to get noticed. In this case, though, it's a great option to do a quick follow up. If you have been able to correspond with the hiring manager, then the pretext for showing up at the office is that since you had been emailing back and forth, you thought you'd like to come in and meet the boss and see what the office looked like.

You can also bring in an updated version of your resume if you have things to add, even if you haven't gotten a response from the hiring manager. One thing you can add to your resume is any progress you've made on technologies they use or new technologies you've pulled into your side projects or open source contributions.

The best time to do this is about a half hour before lunch. Then, while you're chatting with people at the office, you can head out with the group that's going to lunch somewhere and chat with them about work, code, or whatever it is they talk about during lunch.

The type of camaraderie you gain by spending time with people in their downtime will help you build the types of relationships that make them want to help you get hired. And, even if it doesn't work out, they may recommend you to another company that they have friends or former coworkers at if you don't get hired at the company you've targeted.

While you're there, see if they'll let you come in later in the week and spend the day working from one of their desks. It'll give you a good feel for what it's like there. It'll also give them a good feel for what it's like to have you around.

7.6.3 Phone Calls

Phone calls are the most invasive form of follow up—even more than appearing in person. Most people feel like they have to answer their office phone and the connection is more impersonal than a face-to-face visit. If nothing else is working, make a phone call. Try all the other methods of outreach before using the phone.

When you call, ask for the manager or person you need to talk to. Let them know that you've reached out over social media and email. Tell them what you like about them and their company. Then, ask them if they're still hiring or do your follow up on your interview or job offer.

When you call, you don't want to interrupt a meeting or get them when their energy is low. This means that you want to call a couple hours before lunch or right after lunch rather than first thing in the morning when they're likely to have meetings or right before lunch. Also, avoid making the call on a Friday since some folks are prepping to leave for the weekend rather than getting anything done. Their mind won't be on talking to you.

Chapter 8: Getting Noticed

We've walked through the process of building a resume and jumpstarting your job search. You've figured out how to find companies that match up with your dream job.

Sometimes it's difficult to make headway with employees at the companies you're targeting. You have to do something to get noticed. It's also possible that there are great companies out there that line up with your dream job requirements that you're not going to find using our research methods that might notice you if you participate in events and communities in the right way.

Essentially, there are two areas you're looking to be noticed in. Several strategies work well if you're trying to find more companies to target. Many of the rest of the ones outlined in this book work well for getting noticed by people at the company you're targeting.

One objection I get often is from people who aren't comfortable getting publicly involved, speaking with people, or participating in social events. There are definitely levels of involvement you can apply to many of these techniques, but the companies that engage with the community are usually the ones that care the most about the types of employees they hire.

For example, when I was first getting into Ruby and Ruby on Rails, there was a company whose core business was finding leads for colleges. They almost always had the most talented developers working for them. The reason was that several of their developers participated heavily in the Users' Groups. Everyone in the Salt Lake City area knew who they were and how good they were.

This company was also somewhat picky about the skill level and temperament of their employees. So, they'd only invite the qualified people who demonstrated signs that they'd fit into the company well to interview with them. As a result, they had a crack team of developers who worked well together and fit into the culture of challenging each other to grow and writing cutting edge software.

Most companies don't know what they want. This company not only knew what they wanted, but they knew how to screen people in the Users' Groups even if the group's participants didn't know they were being screened.

Applying to a company that knows what kind of employee they want makes your job in getting hired there exceptionally easy, if you fit. It also makes it easy to know if you don't fit because when they say they want something, you know that they mean it.

8.1 Getting Noticed by Companies You're Targeting

We've talked a bit about finding companies and tracking down their employees to make contact. However, there are a few other ways you can stand out as an ideal candidate for these companies. Essentially, these strategies boil down to being around for company discussions, outings, etc.

8.1.1 Co-working From the Office

When I was freelancing, my friend Eric—who actually worked at Instructure—mentioned that they had some free desk space in the office and told me that I was welcome to drop in and work from their office anytime I wanted to. At the time I was coaching a developer named Josh on finding a job. Josh had just graduated from a bootcamp and had applied to Instructure. It occurred to me that many companies that are hiring developers probably already have desk space laid out for them near the team they'd be working on.

If the company is open enough, they're probably just as likely to be happy to have a prospective hire or developer come work from their office a few times to get the lay of the land and figure out if they'd fit in with the development team that sits near them.

This particular approach works better if you're already friends with someone on the team. So, try to line up that phone call or lunch appointment before attempting to work from the company's offices.

That said, while you're at lunch with the developer you've reached out to from the target company, just ask if you can come in and sit at an empty desk and do some open source work. Let them know that you're interested in working for that company and that you want to get a good feel for what it's like to be there.

Then, when you go in, make sure you take your resume and cover letter in—just in case you run into the boss. Also, be sure to get there before lunch and have your new friend introduce you to other members of the team and be present when they get up to head out for lunch.

8.1.2 Going into the Corporate Office

If the company has an office near where you live, you can also just drop by. Typically, showing up unannounced will help you more than it'll hurt you because it shows initiative. This is especially useful if you've been following up every week or so and haven't heard back. Take your resume and cover letter and tell the receptionist that you'd like to quickly hand deliver it to the hiring manager.

I generally advise people to go into the offices about a half hour before lunch time. This sets up your timing so that you finish talking to the boss about the same time that the developers on your prospective team get up to head off for lunch.

When you see people start getting up and talking about where they'd like to eat, introduce yourself and ask if you can go with them.

Some groups of co-workers will talk about work at lunch. However, others turn out to be good friends and will talk about other things while out to lunch. At two of my previous jobs, lunch was a time where we'd alternate between talking about movies, music, and video games and talking about code and how I could get better.

In either case, you have an opportunity to let them see you as a person that has something in common with them in a more casual setting. If they end up liking you or being impressed with you, they may end up asking their boss about you later.

8.1.3 Building Add-ons

If you can't show up at the corporate offices, you can show up on their radar by doing something interesting with the software they're building. Since I've been using Instructure as an example, consider building a plugin for one of their products. They also offer an API that allows you to extend the capabilities of their products to integrate nicely with other systems that do interesting or important things.

If you do a bit of work looking into their social media or support pages, you may find ideas from their customers for integrations you can pull together.

Other companies offer data or APIs that you can use to extend the usefulness of their applications as well. Build a dashboard with their data. Build an integration with a payment system like Stripe or Paypal. Have Trello cards you add to a board you control programmatically added to their system in a new and novel way.

By showing proficiency with the APIs and building something interesting or useful for their clientele, you demonstrate that you understand what they do and a familiarity with their products that they'd have to train other developers on.

8.1.4 Contributing to Corporate Open Source

In addition to plugins and add-ons, you can contribute to any libraries or applications that the company maintains for free for the development community to use. For example, Instructure has an open source version of their Learning Management System, Canvas, that they maintain for people to install and use on their own servers.

The open source version is typically pulled from their paid offering, so, if you wind up contributing features or fixing bugs in the software, you're probably going to be solving a problem that they will pull up into the paid version of Canvas.

Can you imagine having anything better for your resume than a number of contributions to a system that they pay people to work on? The job would basically be yours for the asking.

The other format of Corporate Open Source comes in the form of libraries that companies make available for the general public that do not constitute complete applications. For example, VMWare has an open source Angular component library called Clarity.

Clarity itself isn't a full on application, it's a design system build on Angular. It's used across a number of applications at VMWare. It's been open sourced to allow other companies and developers to use it and to get contributions to it by the wider web development and Angular communities.

Because it's used across VMWare's ecosystem, if you wanted to get a job at VMWare working on some of their products based on web technologies, contributions to Clarity would be a terrific way to get noticed.

How to Contribute

If you're not sure how to get started contributing or don't feel like you have the skills required, don't worry. There are usually plenty of easy ways to get involved.

One of the best ways to get started contributing on an open source projects is to have a look at the issues list on Github.

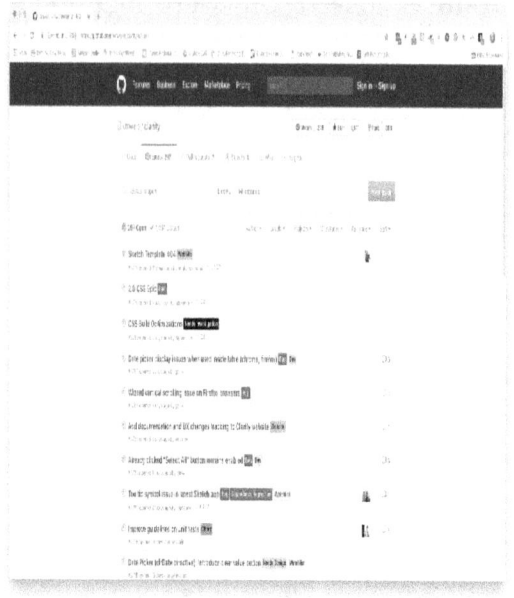

Many open source projects will label issues with a "New Developers" or "Newbies" label. (Clarity doesn't.) If you're considering getting involved with an open source project, this is a great place to start. Just make sure you read any instructions they have for contributing to the project—usually in a CONTRIBUTING.md file on the project—and read the documentation so you understand what the expectations are for getting involved and how the project works.

Another way to get involved is to contribute to the documentation. Read through it and look for any typos. Most documentation is generated from a code repository, so when you find a problem, you can submit a change to the repository in the form of a pull request.

Also, related to documentation, many developers write documentation for the level their at. This means that contributors to the project will gloss over things that will get other folks stuck. So, work through examples highlighting anything you get stuck on and then submit pull requests with clarifications to the documentation.

You can also clarify concepts that you find hard to understand by looking them up or asking questions. Just make sure that you're clear that you're asking to make the documentation more approachable.

Many people have started contributing to an open source project by working on the documentation only to find themselves on the core team of the project contributing code later on.

8.1.5 Attending Corporate Events

I've talked a bit about Instructure in this book. One thing they do every year for their community is put on InstructureCon. InstructureCon is a conference for developers and power users to come learn about the new features of Canvas and their other offerings. They have developer specific talks that you can attend and learn how to customize their products.

I've included a whole section on getting noticed at conferences in the portion about getting noticed by companies you're not targeting. You can use all of those techniques to get noticed at corporate events. The difference is that most of the people running and participating in the event are the people you need to get to know to properly target the company to get hired.

So, if they're putting on this type of event, see if you can volunteer, speak, or use some of those techniques to stand out.

8.2 Getting Noticed by New Companies

As I said before, getting noticed by new companies is mostly a matter of doing something that gets you attention at an event or in a community where employees from those types of companies spend time. These techniques also work if you're targeting a company and can find the events and communities that they spend time in. You may also find that you get noticed by people from one company while targeting another company in this way.

This is because people who are alike often find their ways to the same communities.

The question then becomes: How do I stand out? Let's look at what some of these venues look like and how you can stand out. Generally, though, the best way to get noticed is to do something that demonstrates your expertise and a willingness to learn and to help.

8.2.1 Users' Groups

Users' Groups are gatherings of developers who work with the same or similar technologies and typically bring in developers that work or live in a geographic area. I've found a few jobs and a number of contracts through the Users' Groups I've attended. I've also had a number of jobs come up years after I met someone at a Users' Group when we reconnected and found out where they were at that time.

When you go to a Users' Group, the way to stand out is basically to do anything but sit in the back and not talk to anyone. The strategies provided here start at the most basic and easiest to implement and trend toward the ones that are harder, but yield better results.

Meet People

For the most part, the people you will meet at a Users' Group will be people like you. Some of them will have more experience than you do and some will have less. However, if you're both at the same Users' Group, you already have something in common—an interest in the overarching topic the Users' Group discusses.

When you go to a meeting, sit down next to someone you don't know and introduce yourself. Then ask them how long they've been using the technology that you're there to learn about and ask them where they work. If you get nothing else from the conversation, you'll probably get a new company you can research and target in your job search–or research and eliminate if they don't match up with what you're looking for.

Usually, though, this will be an opportunity for you to make contact with someone who probably uses that technology for a living and get some ideas around what they do and what you can learn to qualify yourself for the job they do at their company.

Besides people sitting in the group at the meeting, make sure to introduce yourself to the speakers after the meeting and let them know what you thought about their talk or demonstration. Give them constructive feedback and ask any questions you made a note of while they were speaking that didn't get asked. This gives you the opportunity to have a conversation with someone who has spent some time learning about a particular topic and an opportunity to build a relationship with someone in the community.

Help Organize Meetings

Many of the people I've coached in getting a job are worried that their technical skills aren't up to scratch when it comes to getting hired. As we've discussed before, many times it's who you know that makes the difference. Plus, organizing a place for people to come, grab food, and talk about technology doesn't require deep technical skills. It only requires a little bit of self confidence and a few minutes on the phone.

The benefits are that the folks who organize the meetings are often approached when a company needs to hire someone. They're also typically well connected with the companies in the area that are willing to host or sponsor a meeting because they talk to them about supporting the community.

Some of these folks aren't very interested in doing the work to call these companies in order to line up a sponsor to buy pizza or to lend out their conference room. They do it because it allows them to get together with their friends from the community and learn something together.

So, if you've attended a couple of meetings of a Users' Group, make it a point to walk up to the organizer and ask them what you can do to help get things together. If you notice that they're having trouble getting speakers or lining up food, ask them who has spoken or provided food in the past and get their phone number when you offer to call, text, or email them.

Also, mention that you're looking for a job. If you can deliver on the food or speakers, you'll be top of mind the next time a company comes to them and asks who they should hire.

Give a Talk

Most people are terrified of the prospect of giving a talk. However, a Users' Group is an extremely forgiving place to do it. They're also usually fairly interested in having people speak on more basic concepts than conferences because they want to attract a wider base of developers.

In the Salt Lake City Ruby Users' Groups, we used to solicit "primers" which were talks that were supposed to be 5 to 10 minutes and covered a basic topic related to Ruby.

Most organizers would be delighted with a monthly talk on the basics. And, if you're the one providing them, you get to be in front of the room as one of the "experts" speaking to the group. In most situations, being a speaker gives you more credibility than being knowledgeable about a specific topic.

Furthermore, as software becomes more complicated, your ability to communicate about what you're doing becomes more important. I've had dozens of development managers express to me that they'd rather hire a good communicator who can learn to be a competent developer than an expert developer who can't communicate with or work with other people.

The age of the lone genius is dead. If you want a programming job today, you need to be able to communicate. Giving talks provides you with practice while developing those skills and a place for you to show prospective bosses and co-workers that you have those skills.

One more pointer here, if you can throw in some fancy shortcut into your presentation while working with your editor, the command line, or something else, that goes a long way toward looking like an expert. I've had a number of people watching a talk ask me how I did something after the talk and act thoroughly impressed even though it amounted to a keyboard shortcut I had set up on my development machine.

Start a Users' Group

If you can't find a group in your area for your chosen area of expertise, start one.

As we've mentioned before, it doesn't have to be anything super formal and doesn't require coding skills. You don't even have to find speakers. Just start getting together on a regular basis and talk about code.

Here's an approach that I've seen work in the past.

First, get on meetup.com and set up a meetup group. Currently, you have to pay to be a group organizer, but it's well worth it if you can connect with other developers in your area. For a location, call or visit local software businesses or co-working spaces. If there's nothing like that that'll work, then schedule the meetup to be held at a local coffee shop or restaurant that won't been too busy at that time of night.

For the agenda of your first few meetings, use some katas or coding exercises like [Conway's Game of Life](#) or [Project Euler](#). You can also follow tutorials on how to build things like twitter bots or clones of popular websites. This approach will help you avoid having to find speakers or delve too deeply into things you're not familiar with. The exercise can be a group exploration of the concepts needed to build the application.

You can also form a group to work through exercises in a book or online course. There are several in my local area working through [FreeCodeCamp](#) together.

Be aware that the first few meetups you have may only get you a few other people coming. However, if you have a good experience, then people will keep coming and will tell other people to come.

In this case, you'll get the benefits of being a group organizer in your local area and start finding opportunities where they were hard to come by before.

8.2.2 Conferences

Conferences have a lot in common with Users' Groups in that there are a lot of developers gathered in person to get some sort of training or to learn something about a technology. There are, however, some meaningful differences.

First, conferences usually run all day for one to several days. This means that people will have to take a break to get meals, prepare for the next speaker, and check in on things at work.

Second, many people travel for conferences. This means that their evenings are generally free and that they're grateful to locals who can show them the best spots to eat, hang out, and work.

Third, conferences generally pull speakers from the wider community. So, you'll have the opportunity to interact with people who speak to and influence the community at large.

To successfully take advantage of a conference, you need to try to be in the right place at the right time. If one of the companies you're targeting has people at the conference, find them and sit by them. If they put on an event, be there. If one of their employees is giving a talk, go up and chat with them afterward.

Local Conferences

If you're attending a local conference, you have a huge advantage over people who aren't. You know your way around and hopefully can recommend some great places to get food during lunch and dinner. You can also recommend any tourist and sightseeing opportunities in the area. Playing the local tour guide is a great way to meet people.

Box 8.1. Playing Local Tour Guide

Salt Lake City used to host the Mountain West Ruby Conference. It's also currently hosts the UtahJS conference, ng-conf—the big Angular conference, React Rally, and RubyHACK. Since I live nearby and spend some time in downtown Salt Lake City, I generally take advantage of the opportunity to invite folks to grab food at my favorite local restaurants.

Back when Mountain West Ruby Conference was being held at the Salt Lake City Library, a few of us would arrange to go to dinner at a local Indian restaurant called Star of India.

These dinners were where I got to know several notable people including Yehuda Katz from the jQuery and Ruby on Rails core teams, Jim Weirich—creator of the Rake CLI utility and about a dozen other Ruby libraries, and several others. At other conferences, I was able to arrange opportunities to talk to other people who they knew and grow my network.

Being local was a huge advantage as we could guide people on a walk through downtown to the restaurant and then back to the library where they could find their way to their hotels.

Even when I'm not in Salt Lake City, though, I'll frequently ask around who wants to go get sushi or some local speciality and then arrange for us all to get there.

Meet the Speakers

Most speakers who are speaking at more than one conference on the same topic know each other. For example, look at the ng-conf speaker lineup and compare it to the Angular Mix or Angular Connect speaker lists? You're going to see some of the same people on several of those lists.

It probably won't surprise you to know that all of those folks know each other and for the most part are friends. So, when they attend any conference talks or hang out in the hallway, they're all hanging out together. This means that if you can ingratiate yourself with any one of them, you'll likely meet the others.

So, if you see one of the speakers in the hallway, go introduce yourself and strike up a conversation. Generally people like to talk about themselves and what they do, so if you do a little research before the conference on the speakers or people you want to meet, you'll have at least a fair bit of stuff to talk to them about. If they've given their talk already, you can talk to them about that too.

If they try to get away by explaining that they're going to meet someone else you'd like to interact with, ask if you can come along since you were looking forward to meeting them too.

When your conversation does eventually wind down, ask them if you can email them later to keep up and ask any questions about their area of expertise. Then get their email address.

I typically follow up that evening or the day after the conference depending on how busy I think they'll be. The reason for that is busy people will forget about you if you don't remind them about what you talked about. A quick note that night will give them some context they can hold onto until you reach out again.

If you meet two interesting people you're not sure know each other, introduce them. This is a great way to build some trust and rapport and will quickly get you into peoples' good graces—even if they already know each other.

Finally, you'll find that a lot of the well known folks at a conference sit together. So, if you sit by them, you're likely to meet other folks who also want to meet them and their friends from other conferences that will drop by to say hello.

Box 8.2. Arrive Early

The first conference I ever attended was Mountain West Ruby Conference. I was so excited to be going that I actually showed up about a half hour early. I parked at the Salt Lake City Library, went in, and sat down. After another 10 minutes other people started to trickle in.

I got up, walked over, and sat next to a large white-haired programmer in the balcony seating above the main auditorium. We started chatting and I asked him if he was familiar with mocking and stubbing while testing Ruby. He said he was and I asked him a few questions about how it worked and how to approach it since I was having trouble making some of the finer points work for me.

He patiently explained what I was doing wrong and helped me understand the deeper concepts of testing. It was rather early in my programming career, and the knowledge was invaluable.

As more people began to arrive, several people came and shook this developer's hand and thanked him for all of his work in the community. I had sat down next to Jim Weirich. Among other things, Jim was the author of the flexmock library and had done extensive work both building mocking systems and helping people understand the concepts in his conference talks.

Simply by showing up early and inadvertently positioning myself next to an expert, I had started a relationship with someone who helped shape my career until he passed away in 2014.

Attend Workshops

Some conferences hold workshops the day before or the day after the conference. Despite the extra cost, they're almost always worth it if it's a topic you're interested in learning. It gives you the opportunity in a controlled environment with an expert instructor to learn the topic.

The instructors are also usually people with deep connections to the community. And, since workshop classes tend to be smaller than conference sessions, it's a great opportunity to build a one-on-one connection with the workshop instructor.

Box 8.3. Vue Workshop at Framework Summit

In October of 2018, I attended the Framework Summit in Park City, Utah. I went up for the first day of the conference, which was the workshop day. I was interested in learning Vue.js—a front-end framework written JavaScript.

I've done a bit of work in Angular and have dabbled with React. I wanted to see why Vue was different.

When I walked into the class, I introduced myself to the instructor and let him know how excited I was to learn about Vue. I also talked to him a bit about what I was doing with Vue. We struck up the beginnings of a friendship.

During the class, I would frequently ask questions. Many of the questions were clarifications of points he was making in the class. A few of them were more along the lines of whether the topic of discussion was the best solution for a problem I was facing in an app I was working on.

Most of the feedback I got was valuable both to me and to my classmates as it cemented the when and why to use particular aspects of Vue.js.

After the workshop and throughout the rest of the conference, we'd exchange friendly waves in the hallway and found another opportunity to chat later about code and building applications. That friendship is likely going to develop into further business opportunities for both of us and I now have another person I can go to when I have questions about Vue.js.

Meet Other Attendees

While at the conference, you may find that you identify with another attendee or attendees who are not on the list of well-known developers. Having conversations with them can often sharpen your thinking or teach you new concepts. It can also help you build relationships with people that will pay off down the line in finding a job.

The best conversations are the ones where everyone learns something.

The easiest way to meet other attendees is to make sure to sit around people you don't know and then introduce yourself during breaks. You can do this during lunch, between talks, or after the conference. Ask them who they are, where they're from, and what they do.

You can also keep an eye out for people you know who are talking to people you don't know. Stop, say "Hello!" and introduce yourself. In many cases, the person you know will introduce you.

As you can imagine, the people who know the most people at the conference will be the organizers. I frequently ambush my friends who organize conferences to get an introduction. Sometimes the person I get introduced to is a sponsor or speaker. Sometimes, they're an attendee. They're almost always interesting people to talk to about what they're working on. That in turn gives me ideas that I can use to produce podcast episodes or technologies I can go play with and learn more about.

Once you meet people and find out who they are and what you have in common, find out what kinds of things they're doing with different technologies. The question that pays off the most here is "Why?" followed by "How?"

For example, imagine you get introduced to someone who is using Docker in an unconventional way. Asking why they're doing something the way they are gives you insight into how they think about Docker and the sorts of problems they're trying to solve. A "Why not?" question you can follow up with is why they're not using some other system that solves the problem in a different way. Then you can dig into how they've set up Docker to solve the specific problem they're running into.

Other areas of interest that aren't technology related are how their team is organized and works together, community issues such as minorities in tech, or upcoming releases of the library or language you both use. You don't have to agree with them on everything either. I rarely completely agree with people on issues like this, but understanding why they approach issues in a particular way helps strengthen my own understanding of particular topics.

Carrying on conversations like this outside of the regular conference schedule is typically called the "Hallway Track" and is a highlight of most conferences I attend.

Box 8.4. Discussing Diversity

At the Framework Summit in 2018, I met a few women who had attended the women and non-binary meetup the night before. We started talking about the event and quickly got into a discussion on women in development communities.

This book is not about that particular subject, so I won't go into too many of the details. However, it turned out that we had both thought about the topic a good deal and were able to find a lot of common ground and to find areas where we didn't exactly see eye-to-eye, but were able to come to understand where the other person might be coming from in their particular views.

In my case, I tend to take a data-driven view of many issues. So, I brought up my concerns about some of the approaches taken by people on this issue and my concern over the lack of real data to back up the approaches.

Her case was colored by different experiences she'd had as a woman coming into technology. In several instances, her experiences and what I had been able to find out through data and conversation with others strengthened a particular point of view.

In other cases, we could both come to an agreement that more data should be collected and then discussed the difficulties in accurately obtaining the data. We also discussed her and others' experiences to try to find our way to what was likely the truth.

We didn't always agree. The conversation could have been fraught with contention and anger, but instead was very constructive in building understanding.

Approaching Speakers

Speakers speak at conferences for a variety of reasons. Most of them do it because they love the technology, the community, and want to help other people out. There is the occasional egomaniac that is it for fame or notoriety, but my experience is that these speakers are few and far between. The real toxic personalities also tend to get weeded out by conference organizers who want their attendees to have a positive memorable experience. Because of this, you should be able to approach the majority of speakers and have an interaction with them that you'll be happy with.

The best time to approach a speaker is right after their talk is over. You can jumpstart the interaction with an insightful question during any Q&A session they have at the end of their talk, but you don't need to do that.

Once the speaker's talk is over, their mind can move on to things other than how their talk is going to go. Their stress levels start to decline and they're generally in a good mood. It's also when the material from their talk is freshest in both your and their mind.

Many speakers will talk with attendees in front of the stage for a few minutes after their talk and then take the conversation into the hallway so the next speaker can get set up. If the breaks are short, they may head straight to the hallway.

Most speakers end up spending 20 or more hours gather information for, arranging, practicing, and then giving their talk. This means that they had to leave some things out of their talk that they wished they could have discussed. It also means that they want you to ask questions so they can talk about something that they're knowledgeable about and have prepared to talk about. In fact, sometimes my question is "What did you have to cut from your talk that you think we should know?" or "What is the next step for people who listened to you speak who want to go to the next level?"

Sometimes I hang around after the talk with no intention other than to let them know that the talk interested me and to see if I can follow later if I have questions. If the talk was interesting, often I'll hang around to see if someone else will ask an insightful question to which I'll have a follow up question and be able to dig deeper on the topic.

Speakers love this kind of interaction because it allows them to help people beyond what the talk was able to do and it allows them to use the expertise they built up while writing their talk.

Approaching Sponsors

Most conferences have some of the costs of running the event covered by sponsors. Some sponsors cover a specific thing like the venue or t-shirts. Others simply want a place where they can set up a table or booth where attendees can drop by and talk with them.

In most cases, sponsors are looking at opportunities to show you what they do and how it can benefit you. This type of marketing isn't a bad thing for you. Often, if you become proficient with their product, you can apply to work for them. You can also use that as a jumping off point to apply to work for their customers.

I usually make it a point to spend an hour or so talking to sponsors, finding out what they're looking for, and then seeing if I can find people who match that description. Connecting people for mutual benefit is a terrific way to get noticed.

Approaching Organizers

Conference organizers are like Users' Group organizers except on a larger scale. They tend to know influencers in the space they're in. They also have the clout to approach the big names and have a real conversation with them, even if it's just about coming to the conference.

I personally have benefitted from being part of the Utah JavaScript community and having some of the local developers be the ones that started ng-conf. I also know the organizers of several of the other local conferences and can usually use those connections to preemptively get introduced to people coming out to the conferences.

They're also typically willing to introduce me to people they're meeting and to sponsors.

During the conference, organizers can get busy in a hurry. One emergency, problem, or scheduled event can have them running off with little notice and they'll become annoyed if you get in their way or take up too much of their time when they need to be doing other things.

However, if you know the organizer, feel free to introduce yourself to whoever they're talking to. Sometimes all you need is to say "I was just walking through and saw you talking to someone. Wanted to see if it was someone I should meet!"

If it's a privileged conversation, they'll usually let you know. If it's not, then you can get introduced to some pretty interesting folks this way.

Volunteering

If you've been to a conference, you'll often see a number of people who have a different colored shirt with the conference logo printed on it that are not the organizers. These folks have generally volunteered to help with the conference.

If you can't afford to get into a conference, volunteering is a great way to get a free ticket. It also puts you on the radar of the organizers. If you do a really excellent job, you'll stand out in their mind.

Volunteering can get you invited to volunteer events, organizer events, and give you opportunities to interact one-on-one with speakers.

One example of this is picking up speakers from the airport. Many times, the speakers will fly in from out of town and need to get from the airport to their hotel. Most speakers simply catch a taxi,

Uber, Lyft, or something similar. They're used to it.

But, imagine the opportunity offered by being the only other person in the car with them. In fact, even if you're not volunteering at the event, you can offer to drive speakers and others from the airport to the conference hotel provided you've rented a car or live in the area.

While at the event, you may wind up answering people's questions or helping them find the session they want to attend or handing out badges to attendees, speakers, and sponsors. You can also volunteer to help with a workshop answering other people's questions or helping run the audio/visual components.

If you find a way to become indispensable, you'll gain a powerful ally who can help you find your next job.

Just don't forget the follow up.

Conference Speaking

Speaking is probably the easiest way to get noticed. You're essentially on the stage exploring a topic you've spent a good deal of time studying in front of a bunch of interested people.

I have been offered jobs after nearly every speaking engagement I've done—especially at the bigger conferences. Most of those job offers have had very little to do with the topic I chose to speak on. Instead, the letter usually specified that they had seen my conference talk, were interested in hiring people, and since I was a speaker, I probably knew what I was doing.

Now, before you let your impostor syndrome speak up, you don't need to delve into the inner workings of the language or framework. You don't need to be able to read machine code. Instead, find some unique take on a hot topic that relates to the technology focus of the conference.

For example, as I'm writing this in 2018, hot topics include Artificial Intelligence, Augmented Reality, home assistants like the Amazon Echo, Internet of Things, etc. Now, imagine that you're attending a conference about JavaScript. You can probably come up with a way to do interesting things in any of those areas with JavaScript.

Another talk idea is talking about an area of pain that everyone runs into. If you can speak about that particular issue, you'll very likely get a speaking invitation.

Also keep in mind that getting a speaking invitation is part your topic, part you, and part the organizers. So, if you've given a similar talk at a Users' Group or another conference, make sure that talk is on YouTube and let the organizers know. If not, any speaking you've done counts in your favor. The reason is that it makes you much less of an unknown quantity to the organizers since they can see you speak.

If you're looking for a job, mention that during your talk. You'll almost certainly have someone approach you.

8.2.3 Contributing to Open Source

Open Source software that is software that is released without the code being compiled or obfuscated somehow. In other words you can see and use the code that makes up the software. Generally, open source software is released with a particular license attached that tells people what they can and can't do with the code.

Code is by definition a creative work that is covered under copyright law—at least in the United States—so when you create it, it's considered to be owned by the developer that wrote it.

Box 8.5. A Quick Lesson on Intellectual Property.

Code is by definition a creative work that is covered under copyright law—at least in the United States—so when you create it, it's considered to be owned by the developer that wrote it.

This is why when a developer is hired, they're usually required to sign an agreement that assigns ownership of the code they're writing to the company they're working for. Without this agreement, the work of the developer is owned and copyrighted by the developer.

Sometimes these copyright agreements are overly broad, so make sure to read them thoroughly to ensure that they only cover things you create for the company as asked by the company.

In open source, most developers retain a copyright on the software they write and then assign a license, which states how, where, and when the code they wrote can be used.

The simplest license I've seen is the MIT license. It states that the software can be used by anyone for anything and that the developer offers no warranty or guarantee of quality.

Other licenses are more restrictive. Make sure you know how the software you're using or writing is licensed.

As a contractor, I typically would provide clients with a non-exclusive unlimited use license. This meant that any tricks or nice bits of code I come up with for one client can be used for another and the client could use the software I wrote for them however they wanted.

Open source contributions demonstrate an understanding of the code being written, the software's usage, and/or a commitment to the community. If you're contributing to an open source project, you'll be making connections and working with other developers all over the world to make the programming ecosystem stronger.

This doesn't mean that you have to be some kind of coding genius or see solutions to big problems. You can actually get started by fixing smaller problems. This includes documentation, typos, small bugs, testing issues, etc. You can find issues in github and figure out how to duplicate them.

We made a lot of suggestions in the section on contributing to corporate open source. Those same lessons still apply, the primary difference being that you'll be making connections with private individuals working around the world on the same problem. They, in turn, may be able to introduce you to companies that you're interested in working for.

You can also add open source contributions to your resume. Having higher profile contributions or projects on your resume will help you stand out.

8.2.4 Building a Media Platform

A number of friends of mine have gotten job offers out of the blue by putting content out to the public. I got my second programming job because I sent in a resume that included links to my screencasts online. When I went freelance, I listed my phone number on the website with my screenshots and got more than one call out of the blue from people looking for Ruby on Rails developers.

As a podcaster, whenever I'd finish a contract without another one lined up, I'd mention that I was free for work and would get a handful of phone calls or emails from interested people.

Having a media platform is a great way to build interest in you as a potential employee or contractor.

This isn't a book on building a media platform, but I will go over some of the pros and cons of building a particular type of platform and give some general guidelines regarding how to use them to get interested employers to reach out to you.

General Advice on Building a Media Platform

There are three main keys to building media platforms: Consistency, quality, and marketing. Consistency is by far the most important. Being consistent in posting content will help you build up a library of content that people will want to consume. It makes it more likely for you to hit on a topic that more people care about. It also keeps people coming back to your website for more, which gets you a following that can get you a job.

Quality applies to both your content—good writing, relevant content, etc.—and your medium—video or audio quality. People will tolerate low quality recordings for great content to a certain point, but if it's really hard to hear or watch, they'll turn it off in favor of something else.

A great place to learn what people are searching for is through conversations with them at events. You can also use SEO tools like <u>Google Keyword Planner</u> or a paid option like <u>ahrefs</u>.

It's also easier to build an audience and get attention if you can get the word out.

Posting to social media works only if you already have a social following. Some people will find it there if they don't follow you, but most won't. Instead, make sure to post it to sharing sites as well as social media sites. That way people who find it can share it easily on their social media.

Also, if your content gets traction, it might be featured in a newsletter or other larger publication and gain you even more traction. Find out where people in your particular arena post their content, then make sure that every post, episode, or video gets put up there. Then, if you hit a home run on your quality, you can pick up some new subscribers.

Blogging

Blogging is probably the easiest way to build a platform. You don't need a camera, microphone, or anything else to do it. Instead, all you need is a place to post and an idea to write about.

Early on in my career, I'd write about whatever I was working on. So, I wrote about learning how to test my applications. I had lists of gems I was using for different purposes. I wrote about different obstacles and triumphs in my coding journey. There are all kinds of things you can write about that people a step or two behind you on your coding journey can pick up and learn from.

These days I'm writing about whatever I'm exploring for my next book or course.

One advantage to blogging that the other platforms lack is that Search Engine Optimization is still primarily a text game. The search engines haven't completely mastered sifting through audio or video to properly index those media in a way that will accurately identify keywords that people will be searching for to find that content.

So, in a very real way, podcasters, videographers, and screencasters have to do some form of summary blogging alongside their other content.

The disadvantages basically will boil down to you and your personality. If you're the kind of person who can more naturally speak into a microphone or camera, blogging can feel a bit like a slog.

Personally, the reason I blog as infrequently as I do is because I'm much more natural behind a microphone and I tend to overthink what I'm writing when I'm sitting at a keyboard. Writing this book has gotten me past a lot of that, but it's still a thing. I tend to want to polish my blog posts until they're out of date.

The blog posts that have gotten me the post traffic in the past have been the ones where I've solved a specific problem, posted a specific error message format, and listed a solution. They stand out from the crowd and provide a direct answer to an immediate problem.

I also recommend Darren Rowse's **31 Days to Build a Better Blog** course for how to get started and get traction. Then just be consistent.

You can also get set up with a blog fairly quickly on a host like Bluehost using WordPress.

Podcasting

Given my journey, this is probably the medium you expected me to start with and is likely the one I have the most to say on. That said, this is not a book on podcasting, so you'll get a basic treatment of podcasting. I've been recording and producing podcasts since 2009.

For our discussion here, I'm going to limit the discussion to audio only. You can record and distribute video, but generally it's still a produced conversation even if it's one sided.

I latched onto podcasting because I was a people person and I had the opportunity to talk to really interesting people doing something I really loved to do—write Ruby.

If you're excited about code and it's more natural for you to talk about it that write about it or demo it, then podcasting is probably the way to go. You can flip on your microphone and start talking.

You can worry about some of the other details later. For example, setting up the website, getting album artwork done, etc. can be postponed. For now, just get some content recorded and figure out how it fits in with the larger picture of what you want to talk about and how you want people to see you.

One advantage that podcasting has is that people can hear your voice. They feel like they get to know you a little by how you talk about things and what you talk about.

Your listeners can also listen to you while they're in the car, walking the dog, or mowing the lawn.

Video

Video is split into two parts. There's screencasting, which is essentially recording your screen while you're doing something–like writing code. And there's vlogging—I hate that term—which is you talking into a camera and can be somewhat similar to podcasting with a video component.

Savvy marketers will tell you that Google is the largest search engine in the world and that YouTube is the second largest.[1]

My friend John Sonmez built up a huge audience by blogging on SimpleProgrammer.com and then grew it by moving to YouTube and talking about topics that programmers were interested in there.

I got started by publishing screencasts to TeachMeToCode.com and grew an audience from there through podcasting.

Recording videos has some of the same advantages as podcasting in that people can see you and hear your voice if you're sitting in front of the camera. They get to see what you're capable of and how you work if you're recording screencasts.

Some videos, where the video component is not integral to the message in the video can be converted to audio only and released as a podcast. Others, like screencasts require you to have a screen in front of you to make sense of what you're seeing.

8.2.5 Online Communities

In Utah, we have Users' Groups that operate mostly online. The Ruby and JavaScript groups operate primarily on a Google Group and on Slack. I've been a member of other communities online that use forum software or some other method of communicating. In fact, these days, it seems like an invitation is out for some new group focused on some new thing on a regular basis.

So, assuming you've either targeted a company that has an employee who is actively involved in that group or the group covers a topic you'd like to pursue as part of your career, you're going to want to get noticed there so you can parley your participation into access to the right people.

Be Active

In order to get noticed, it helps if you become a known quantity. If people have seen your name buzz by on the list or in the forum, they're more likely to give you a chance to capture their attention.

Generally this means that you've got to post at a minimum a few times a week and more often if you can.

Make sure that your contributions are relevant and timely. The best way to do this is to answer questions others pose in the group. If you're highly experienced, you can simply answer based on what you've lived through or studied up on. If you're not highly experienced, you can still answer by doing research and then formulating a response.

For example, imagine that someone asked you how to set up authentication in a Ruby on Rails application. If you've done it before, you may recommend a gem—Ruby library—that handles authentication for Ruby on Rails applications like devise. You could explain how you did it and what you ran into with your particular case if you had to do something non-standard while setting it up.

If you're not experienced, you could still link up to a tutorial video on how to set up devise. You could find the documentation where the gem author explained how to set up the gem. You could run through it yourself and tell them where you got stuck and what you did to fix it.

Either way you answered the question in a helpful way. In the second example, you didn't need to be an expert.

There are several other things you can do to remain relevant that don't require expertise. Here are a few other ideas:

Find a blog post or conference video you like. Write up a quick summary of why you found it interesting and post to the group asking what they think. You'll get the conversation rolling and can share further insights while you learn from other developers.

When someone asks a question that is not clear, ask the clarifying questions to get to the main point they're needing help with.

As you build out a side project, ask questions about what you're running into. Get advice on how you've designed or built it. Ask for a 20 minute code review.

All of these kinds of participation will give you chances to interact with others in the group and will get your name or username up there often enough for people to begin to recognize you.

Getting Personal Attention

Once you've been involved in the community for a while or if you'd helped someone out who has some connections you'd like to explore, then you can reach out and see if they'd be willing to meet you for lunch or hop on a call as we've discussed before.

Gary Vaynerchuk has a book called "Jab, Jab, Jab, Right Hook" that talks about the idea that you provide quality content or help over and over again before asking for something. In your case, I recommend you give value over and over again before you ask for the meeting. Generally, this means waiting until you've helped someone three or four times directly or participated in making the conversation in the group better for a few weeks before taking this approach.

You're also welcome to periodically mention that you're looking for a job. If you strike the right chord with someone in the group and the topic of hiring a new developer comes up at work, they may think of you because you brought up your job search.

8.2.6 Hack Nights and Hackathons

Hack Nights and Hackathons are a great place to show off what you can do. Typically, hack nights are opportunities for you to get together with other developers and work on projects that you or they have in the works. Most hack nights start out with one or two people stating that they're going to work on a code kata or some other toy project where others are welcome to jump in.

If someone in that group is someone you want to connect with, then join that group and try to be as close to the action as you can—where you can ask questions, clarify talking points, and contribute to the code.

If you're not interested in that group, it's the perfect time to step up and ask folks to come help you work on your side project. It's a little intimidating to take the lead sometimes, but it's worth it. You'll get to lead the conversation and show off what you've been working on at the same time.

You can also mention that you'd love to have more advanced developers come help you level up on your code, which may signal someone who is interested in mentoring to come join you. This is a prime opportunity because you'll be talking to and working with someone who is a great candidate as a co-worker since they're already willing to mentor other developers.

Hackathons are a little different. They tend to be a place where people form up into teams to build applications that will be judged as part of a competition. It's also a terrific place to get to know people in more depth and really shine if you can deliver in a short timeframe.

Imagine that you and your team build a time management application. If it places, you'll have the opportunity to talk to the other participants as a standout developer for the event. This gives you the opportunity to mention that you're looking for a job. Since you proved that you're a tough competitor, they'll take you seriously as they consider whether or not to refer you to the company they work for.

If you're not the winner, you still get to work closely with 2-5 other developers on a project. They'll get the opportunity to see what you can do and what you have to contribute to the team, both in the code and as a member of the team. This is valuable insight for a prospective boss or co-worker. They'll be able to tell their boss not only what you'll contribute, but why they'd like you on their team.

Also, make it a point to get to know the judges after a hackathon as they're typically chosen for their experience and for being somewhat well known in the local community. They're probably well connected and if they liked your project, they may be able to refer you to some companies that you'd like to work for.

1. https://www.searchenginejournal.com/seo-101/meet-search-engines/ ↑

Chapter 9: Winning Interviews

Once you've gotten noticed and been called in for an interview, you're ready for the next stage. I like to compare interviews to sales calls. If this turns you off a little, let me explain how I approach sales.

Sales calls are an opportunity for you and your customer—or in this case the potential employer—to figure out how you can mutually benefit each other. In the salesperson's case, it's a matter of what they'll pay for the product. For the customer or employer, it's what the product—in this case, you—can contribute to what the employer is trying to accomplish.

In other words, don't think about interviews as a chance to convince someone to hire you. You don't need to prove anything. Instead, your goal is to demonstrate to the employer what you can contribute to them in the way of software and soft skills and to figure out if they're offering you a place you'd like to work and opportunities to grow and build toward what you want from your career and your life.

I've talked to people who wanted to work for huge companies like Facebook and Google as contributing members of teams that build software that changes the world. I've also talked to people who wanted to collect a paycheck and be home at five o'clock. There are also people who want to get in on the ground floor of a startup and help build its culture and customer base.

None of these are wrong. You may start out thinking that you want one type of career, working for a Google-like company, and figure out that you really do want a more intimate team than a corporate environment. You may go from wanting a paycheck and home-at-five lifestyle to craving the challenge and opportunities you get at work every week. Keep exploring until you know what lights you up, and then decide when it's time to make your current position into that next thing or when it's time to move on.

In the meantime, at the interview, if you're clear about what you want right now and clear about what you bring to the table, then you and the person you're interviewing can evaluate how well you and the company fit each other.

9.1 A Few Notes of Caution

There are a few things you should not do at an interview. I'm going to go through that list now because you can either blow the interview or hurt yourself in salary negotiations if you do them.

First, don't disclose your salary requirements. After talking to and coaching dozens of developers into getting jobs, I've learned one thing. Whatever salary you ask for will be the salary you get. I'm sure you're thinking "Chuck! How is that a bad thing?!" Let me explain. When you walk into that room, the company already knows how much they want to pay someone in your position. Usually, it's a range with a minimum and maximum. If you ask for anything less than the maximum, that's the offer you'll get—even if your offer is below the minimum.

Instead, ask what the salary range is for the position. Some companies will defer telling you that information. If they do, let them know that's fine and that you'll look forward to their offer letter.

If they insist that HR or some other department needs that information in order to put you into the system, tell them that you understand, but that your career coach told you that you'd be compromising your ability to negotiate later if you did so. Tell them that if HR needs a number to put in whatever the top of the salary range is for that position and that you can negotiate once they send you an offer letter.

Second, don't complain. Period. There are two natural outcomes from complaining. First, you come off as negative. Unless the person who is interviewing you was there when whatever you're complaining about took place, they have no idea what the context is. All they have to go on is your tone. Their impressions of the interview after the fact will also be tainted by the negativity.

Sometimes this is hard because what happened to you was legitimately awful and wrong. However, unless they were there, they won't understand.

The other reason to avoid complaining is that the savvy interviewer will read into your complaints that you may be prone to complain about them or your teammates. You may not be that kind of person, but they won't know that by spending a half hour or so with you. Negative people and complainers are hard on a team and can also sometimes cause larger problems within the company for their boss.

Box 9.1. How to Blow a Phone Screening

In 2017, I put in a job ad for someone to come help me manage the production of the podcasts and help with scheduling and promotion. I listed the job on a local jobs board and then proceeded to begin qualifying over 200 people.

The first thing I did was have the candidates use a scheduling link to schedule themselves a phone screening. Then, I spent 3 days on the phone doing over 90 phone screenings.

My phone screenings usually start with who they are and what they want. Then I dive into their qualifications. Then I ask them what their former bosses and coworkers would say about them. Since calling references is part of my process, I warn them that I'll be reaching out to their past bosses after I talk to them. This typically gets me some pretty candid responses.

One candidate I got on the phone with had run her own business in the past. As I talked to her about her qualifications, I got more excited. She knew how to get done most of what I needed. This was my dream employee.

She failed her phone screening when I asked her what her former bosses would say about her. She started out by complaining about what an idiot her first boss had been. Given that the business had failed—according to her—due to incompetence, she was probably right. But, she was extremely negative about her boss and the entire situation. Then she told me about her next boss and how that boss had messed up more stuff. Then she started a karate dojo. Her business partner there had apparently sexually harassed her. They were in a lawsuit and I got the full explanation of what he had done to her.

After we got off the phone, I took her off my list. Here's where her problems were.

First, I was going to be her next boss if I hired her. I'm happy to take feedback, but I knew I'd end up firing her if she was talking about me like I was some kind of idiot behind my back. Not because I have an ego, but because I couldn't count on her not doing that with my customers if she was willing to do so over the phone with me—a complete stranger.

Second, while she sounded extremely credible explaining the harassment she had received, I wasn't certain that if I deeply offended her that she wouldn't do everything she could to destroy my business. I've deeply offended someone in the past that I had to let go. That person worked for about 3 months to tear me and my business down and I worried that this person carried the same risk.

Here's what she should have done...

First, she should have explained how she had tried to save the failing business instead of complaining about her boss. This would have gone a long way to convince me that she would put in hardcore work for me. She could have explained that she and her boss didn't see eye-to-eye on some things and how she constructively dealt with that.

Second, she was so consumed by what her business partner had done that she tried to tear him down. I understand that it's got to be an emotional thing to be treated the way she was. I really don't blame her for being upset. Honestly, it made me want to go punch the guy out. However, knowing that I was likely going to call him as a past boss or business partner, she should have stated that they were in a law suit over his sexual harassment and left it there.

I don't want to demean what she went through, but I want to demonstrate that no matter how bad it was, complaining will hurt your chances more than it helps.

Finally, be prepared. If this sounds like strange advice–after all, the interview is where they ask you about yourself—keep in mind that if you're ready to answer specific questions, you can cast yourself in the best light. Especially in phone screenings where you have limited time to give an answer, if you're already prepared to discuss what they're asking about you can get the point across quickly and succinctly. You can also practice talking about some of the things they'll ask you about that are your weak points.

For example, if you have an answer prepared for "Looking at your resume, it doesn't appear that you have a lot of experience" you can help them understand that you learn quickly and fill in some of the gaps regarding things you've worked on outside of what's on the resume.

Being prepared also means making sure you have enough time for the interview. Ask them how long the interview takes so you can block out the time and make sure you don't have to leave early.

9.2 Phone Screenings

You won't always be asked to participate in a phone screening. Phone screenings are a tool for hiring managers to quickly weed people out who aren't a great fit. In other words, they're looking for a reason not to call you in for an interview.

When you think about it, this makes sense. Why spend a half hour or so with someone trying to determine if they're a good fit for the company if you can rule them out in 5 minutes? You save yourself hours of time! Plus, if you have a large pool of potential employees, this narrows the field before you get stuck on someone because they have an impressive resume.

There are generally two ways phone screenings can go. Either the hiring manager knows what they're looking for and will ask targeted questions, or they don't and won't.

If they don't have targeted questions, then you just have to make it through a 5 minute conversation without raising any red flags. Make sure that you emphasize what you like about their company to demonstrate that you prepared for the phone screening and be honest about where you're at in your coding journey. Give them as much of an opportunity to get to know you as possible.

For the more targeted types of phone screenings, start by looking on GlassDoor to see if there's any information about the phone screenings. If you can find out what they're going to ask you, you can prepare better for the screening. If there's no such information, then make sure your resume is handy since some of the things they'll ask you about will likely come from their brief reading of your resume and cover letter.

For all phone screenings, make sure that you're in a quiet place where you can easily hear them and where they can hear you.

Box 9.2. Phone Screening at Walgreens My all time favorite phone screening story was when I was calling around to fill that podcast producer position. I schedule 10 minute phone screenings back to back, so when I got asked if I could call him back in 10 minutes over the sound of his car door closing, I told him that I had someone else scheduled in 10 minutes.

"Oh, well, I'm at Walgreens. This really isn't a good time."

I thought to myself If this wasn't a good time, then why did you schedule it for this time of day?.

I told him it was now or never.

He walked into the store with his phone to his ear and picked up whatever it was he was looking for. I asked him my first two questions while he wandered around.

"Hang on for a second!" he said as I heard the Walgreens checker greet him.

"Sorry, I'm not going to hang on for a second. Obviously you're not serious enough about this job to take this phone screening seriously. I'm gonna hang up now, OK?"

He used some foul language to tell me what he thought about me hanging up. Then I hung up.

If you want to ace a phone screening, make it clear that you took it seriously and that you were waiting for their call.

9.2.1 Regular Interviews

Most interviews consist of technical questions, some form of a coding exercise, and personal evaluations designed to see how well you fit into the company and team. Because of the differences between companies, there's no guideline that will fit all interviews for all companies.

You'll also find that—as we've said before—some companies really know what they want, others don't know what they want beyond another pair of hands to help carry the load. For the first, if you can figure out what they're looking for, you can tailor your answers to help them see that you're a match for their criteria. For the latter, you're appealing to whatever it is hiring manager gets most excited about that makes them want to work with you.

For this section, I'm going to start preparing for the interview and move up to the actual interview and following up. Refer to Chapter 4 for how to research companies and find out what they're looking for.

Dress Up One Level

When I coach developers on interviewing, the most common question is some variation on "What should I wear?" Some folks worry that wearing a shirt and tie or a skirt is overdressing. Others don't want to dress up because it's not what they'd wear to work and they don't want to work at a place that has a stringent dress code.

Generally, my advice is to dress one level above whatever the norm is at the company. So, if they're generally in faded jeans and a t-shirt, then wear a nice dark pair of jeans and a polo shirt or nice blouse. If they lean toward the dress pants and polo shirt, then a nice pair of slacks or a nice skirt and a button down shirt or higher end blouse is probably the ticket.

You don't have to go to a ton of trouble in how you dress, but edging it up a bit lets them know that you're taking the interview seriously. Just make sure that it's something comfortable so that you look natural when you're wearing it.

Arrive Early

When you go to the interview, do what you can to arrive 10 minutes early. This gives you a bit of leeway if you run into traffic or encounter some other delay.

You can quickly deal with it and still be on time.

Don't walk in more than 5 minutes early. The interview is the opening of negotiations for salary and other benefits on the job. If you arrive more than 5 minutes early, it makes you appear over eager to get the job and sends the message that you don't have better things to do with your time.

Be Confident

Once you arrive, make sure that you're showing confidence. Keep in mind that if they didn't already think you could do the job, they wouldn't have invited you in for an interview. You're also not competing with the other applicants. You're working with them to determine if you and they are a good fit. So, clearly and boldly let them know who you are and then let them decide if you're the kind of person they want to hire.

Be Honest

In nearly every interview you go to, you'll be asked a question about something you don't know enough about. Saying "I don't know" is not a deal killer. In fact, most people don't want to work with a know-it-all. It's not just the interpersonal aspects of dealing with someone who knows everything either. It's also that people who don't ask for help or look up answers tend to make major mistakes that others have to fix.

Better than I don't know is an explanation of what you do know and how you'd find the answer using Google or Stack Overflow.

I've never used that library before, but I'm pretty sure that quick Google search on how to set up encryption with that library would get to a great Stack Overflow answer that I can modify to make it work.

You may also be asked questions about items on your resume or personal life that you're not comfortable disclosing. For some personal details, you're not required to disclose them. For example, religion, political affiliation, and family size or composition are things you shouldn't have to disclose unless you're applying to a particular religious, political, or other group where that's relevant. In those circumstances, you can provide those answers if you think it'll help you or respond with "I'd rather not discuss that."

For other things where you need to provide an answer such as talking about past mistakes at previous jobs, exposing personal weaknesses, or past criminal records, be honest and be clear about what you've learned from those experiences as well as what you've done to make sure those issues are behind you.

You can be honest about negative things and still come out on top.

Ask Questions

Work off your Top 3 to make sure that the company is a great fit for you. Let them know what the big issues for you are and then ask them how they approach those things. For example, if salary is in your Top 3, ask them how they make salary determinations.

Box 9.3. Salary at Basecamp

In a Ruby Rogues podcast interview with David Heinemeier Hansson—creator of Ruby on Rails and co-founder of Basecamp—David told us how he hires and sets salary at Basecamp.

David told the Rogues that he likes hiring junior and mid-level developers that he can train to work the way they do at Basecamp. This generally goes against conventional wisdom that dictates that you hire experienced people who can take on your problems and apply their experience to it. This opens the debate on whether experience or how you work is what is key.

He also mentioned that he pays developers based on the going rate of a developer at their level in Chicago. This means that if they live in some other area of the United States or another country, they'll still get paid a competitive wage for the Chicago area. It also flattens the pay structure across the entire company and adjusts depending on what the market for software developers does.

This illustrates the need to ask questions and keep in mind that not everyone does things the same way.

If benefits are in your Top 3, then get clear on what benefits they offer and what companies they use to administer them. Then you can go home and do some research to make sure that they cover the doctors and treatments you care about or determine if the days off offered are sufficient.

You should also ask if you can see where you'd be working and meet the team you'd be working with. Remember that this is a chance for you to find out if they fit you as much as for them to see if you fit them.

Find out what hours they expect you to be around.

Box 9.4. Out of Sight, Out of Mind

I ran into a problem at my first job as team lead of the development team. One of our developers would come in to work early so he could leave early and be home for his kids when they got out of school. The CEO was the type that would sleep in until 11am, go golfing and pick up lunch before arriving at the office around 1pm or 2pm.

After about a month, the CEO came to me and told me to fire the developer who was coming into work early. He explained that he wasn't willing to pay someone's salary if they were never in the office.

I was forced to sit down with the CEO and explain that not only was the developer putting in extra hours, but that he was a critical part of what we were trying to accomplish at that company. I also asked if he'd like this developer to start coming in a little later and staying a little later. This was ultimately one part of what we agreed on.

The next week that developer began coming at 8am and leaving at 5pm.

Getting clear expectations about this up front is important when it matters.

Incidentally, that developer wound up leaving a month or two later because expectations hadn't been set and then had been changed in a way that didn't work for him.

A few other questions to ask are:

- How do you decide what to work on next?
- Are there certain areas of the code that certain developers

> have some form of ownership over?
> - What kinds of problems are you looking to have me solve?
> - Do you provide opportunities for developers to learn, level up, and interact with other industry developers?
> - How do you determine if a feature has been implemented completely and correctly?

The more you know about how the company and team operate, the better you can determine fit or ask for different arrangements as part of your salary negotiation.

Follow Up

Interviewers, HR personnel, and team leads are busy people. Often, the reason you don't hear back from them is because they're waiting to interview that one last person or because they got bogged down with other work. Ask them at the end of the interview when you should expect to hear back. Then ask if you can call them if you don't hear back by that date.

When you call, be courteous, but get straight to the point. "Hi, I just wanted to check in. You said I'd hear back by today and I'm still interested in working for you."

You may hear that they hired someone else, or this may be the initiative that gets you a job offer. About half the time, the people I've coached have gotten job offers the same day they made this call.

9.3 Technical Screenings

When people think about the interview process, this is the part most people think of. This section of the interview can come in a number of different forms. You may be asked a series of technical questions to see how well you know the libraries and tools used in writing software. You may be asked to sit down and code with someone. Or, you may be asked to write code in front of a group.

9.3.1 Coding Sessions

Many employers have gone to a model where they sit down with candidates and have them work through a coding exercise to see how they work. Most of the time, they want to see that you have a baseline command of the language or framework and to see how you approach solving problems.

They're almost never set up to stump you. Usually, they're aimed at seeing where your limits are and how quickly you are able to overcome them.

If you've written a good amount of application code already, then you will have encountered instances where you don't know the solution to a problem off the top of your head. Or, if you know what pattern to use, you may not know exactly how to implement it front to back.

If this is the case, then the coding exercises should be relatively easy for you since you'll simply find the answers you need on the internet. What you'll demonstrate is that you have enough of the right skills to quickly identify the answer on the internet and put it into practice in your application.

Performing large or complicated solutions off the top of your head is impressive, but unless you've already practiced at them, focus on being good at finding and implementing solutions.

Also be prepared to answer questions about why you're approaching the problem with a specific solution and answer any technical questions that come up.

Mastering this type of interview is mostly about practice. Find some programming exercises and smaller apps you may be asked to work on during an interview and work through them. Do them multiple times before you arrive using different approaches, techniques, and constraints so you can intelligently discuss why you do or don't use a specific solution.

If they give you a take home assignment, the faster you turn it in, the more impressed they'll be. "Build us a blog" is a common request. Make sure to ask them enough questions that you understand what features they want and any other constraints they have for these projects.

Whiteboard Coding

One common interviewing practice is to hand an applicant a whiteboard marker and have them write code on a whiteboard. This is essentially a way to make them perform under pressure with no help from the internet.

When I'm hiring developers, I never use this method because I want to see how they react under pressure in a situation that looks much more like the conditions they'd be working under. I also have better ways to add stress to the interview that tell me more about the applicant than whiteboards do.

That said, it's a common enough practice that you need to know how to handle it.

Above all, stay calm. Many applicants start getting agitated when they don't know an answer and aren't sure what to do. If you're not sure that you can stay calm in the face of a whiteboard interview, have a friend come in and criticize you while you're doing whiteboard coding until you can do it calmly.

When you don't know the exact syntax, function, or method for doing a thing just say so. Telling them that "I know there's a function that finds the average of an array of numbers, but I can't remember what it is. So, since I can't look it up, I'm just gonna use a function called 'average().'" Then write it up on the board.

If fact, writing general statements instead of code if you don't know the exact syntax is called pseudocoding is fairly common in whiteboard interviews.

You may also ask if they're OK letting you look things up on your phone since you're not coding at a computer.

Box 9.5. Turning a 'No' into a 'Yes'

When I was working for Mozy, they had a developer named Jacob come in and do an interview. I walked by the room where they were grilling him on the whiteboard a couple of times. Then, they sat him down in my office and had him work in the corner to build a blog using Ruby on Rails.

They had given him a specific number of features to add and after a few hours, someone came in and told him that his time was up.

He committed his code to Github and then walked out to the bad news that since he hadn't finished the blog, he wasn't going to get the job.

I could tell that he was discouraged as he walked out the door.

The next morning around 10:00, Jacob walked back into our office. He asked to see Jon, the team lead who had not hired him the day before. He and Jon talked for a bit, got on a computer, and after a while Jacob left again. He had gotten Jon to change his mind and hire him.

I wound up chatting with Jon a little later in the day and asked what Jacob did to change his mind.

"He finished the blog last night," Jon said.

"But he didn't get it done in time..." I responded. I knew that Jon wasn't a pushover.

"Yes, but he was making sure he did it right and he was up half the night finishing it."

It was clear to me, then that what Jon wanted more than a coding wizard who could sling code on the whiteboard and bust out a blog in an afternoon was someone he could rely on.

9.3.2 Answering Technical Questions

Beyond coding exercises, sometimes you'll get questions about programming that are designed to see how much you know. They'll go deep in some areas and just make sure you're passable in others.

As with the whiteboard and coding exercises, stay calm. Most of the time these questions aren't designed to stump you or trip you up. They're designed to see how far your knowledge goes and see how you respond when you're don't know.

Preparation is the key here. Most of the time you can talk to people who have interviewed at or work for the company and find out what kinds of questions they like to ask in advance. Glassdoor.com also has a lot of the interview questions that get asked.

Find out what they are and then take the time to learn the answers. Learning the answers isn't just a matter of knowing that this library provides that functionality. Dig deep. Find out why people use it. Figure out why it's built in a particular way. What design philosophies went into it? A good interviewer will try to find out how deep your knowledge runs.

You should also be sure not to make things up. An employee that isn't willing to admit that the don't know something is an employee that is likely to make a stupid mistake or invent an unmaintainable mess instead of asking for the right solution. Most employers are looking for results, not novel solutions.

Chapter 10: Salary Negotiations

Once you've gone through a company's interview process, if they want to hire you, the company will extend an offer with salary, benefits, and other details.

As with interviews, entire books have been written about negotiating salary. My favorite one is <u>Fearless Salary Negotiation</u> by my friend Josh Doody. He walks you through the process of getting the highest salary you can.

I intend to guide you through the process, but can't be as thorough in one chapter as he is in an entire book.

10.1 Know Your Numbers

The best way to walk into a salary negotiation prepared is to have information. You need to know what the market is paying developers who have the same level of experience and skills that you do. We walked you through finding salaries in Section 3.2. You also need to know what you want or need to make.

When you come up with a salary number, start out with your personal expenses. You can use a tool like YNAB or Mint to figure out how much you spend every month. Or, you can put together a basic spreadsheet and estimate what each expense is and what you pay for it. Since you can import bank information to both systems, I recommend you use YNAB and import your bank information to get a good idea of what your spending looks like based on actual data.

Once you know how much you spend each month, you can multiply the total by twelve to get an accurate picture of what your yearly salary needs to be just to meet your basic needs. Then you can adjust your salary based on the salary data you gather online.

You should walk away with two numbers: what you'd like to make and the minimum salary you are willing to accept. For the second number, do not compromise on that number. If you can't negotiate higher than your minimum salary, then you have to be willing to walk away. If after a few negotiations you're not getting your minimum, you may reconsider. But you have to fail negotiations at least three times before you adjust that number. Some companies are out to get a deal on salaries instead of being out to get great talent.

10.2 Make Then Give You the First Number

During an interview or on a job application—like an online form—you'll be asked for a salary requirement. Every time I've given a company that number, that's the amount I got offered. I've always wondered if, for those jobs, if I had waited to see what they were willing to pay, I could have gotten a better salary. In one case, I had to make all my performance bonuses to get the salary I asked for.

If they were willing to pay what I asked for right out of the gate, how much more could I have asked for that they would have given me in order to get me on board? Would they have happily paid an extra $5,000 per year? $10,000 per year? more?

Keep in mind that whatever number is put forward first is the number that all later stages of the negotiation start from. You see this in movies and TV shows often, where the first mover offers an extreme lowball offer. Then the counter comes in with a highball offer. Then they settle somewhere in the middle.

Salary negotiations aren't quite as dramatic, but they follow the same general pattern. If you put forward an offer and it's in their price range, they'll take it. If you're too high or they think they can talk you down, they'll counter with a lower number. Usually there are only one or two counter offers before people settle on a salary.

Most companies have a range they're willing to go to for salary. Ask for it. When they've given you a number to work from aim for the top of their range for your salary. You can also give up on companies that are not above your minimum salary. Just make sure you let them know that's why you're no longer interested in interviewing or working for them. They may surprise you with better offer.

When pressed, just let them know that you're happy to negotiate when they give you a job offer, but since you don't know what their salary range is, you're not comfortable telling them what yours is.

10.3 Making a Counter Offer

If you wait until they give you a number, you're almost always going to be waiting until they extend an offer. Traditionally, this comes in an offer letter, but sometimes you'll get a phone call with the offer details. This is the point at which you can—and should—counter offer.

Most of the people I've coached have countered an offer with either a 10% increase or by increasing to the next increment of $10,000 salary. For example, a $55,000 per year salary offer could be countered with $60,000 per year to get to the next $10,000 increment or $60,500 by adding 10%. In either case, it gives the company room to counter back and in about half the cases, the company simply accepts the new number and hires the person.

By the time you get an offer from a company, someone over there has become somewhat emotionally invested in getting you on board. Because of this, countering an offer is pretty safe.

Besides that, companies expect at least one counter offer and won't rescind an offer because you countered their offer. Because of this, there's almost no downside to putting forward at least one counter offer. Even two or three counter offers isn't an unreasonable series of events as you narrow down what is acceptable to both you and the company. As long as they don't feel like you're trying to nickel and dime them, which can happen if you continually push for that last concession.

Generally, I recommend that people counter once on salary. If the company accepts your counter offer, the negotiation is finished. If they counter your offer with a lower salary that is acceptable to you, then give another counter offer that includes better benefits.

If the salary they countered with is unacceptable, then let them know what your firm minimum is and let them decide if it's worth it to them.

10.4 Negotiations Are Not Just on Salary

Salary is cumulative—meaning that your next salary will often have some basis on your previous salary. Even if it's you that's basing your minimum salary on your last salary. Most companies will offer you a percentage raise on your current salary if they know what it is when hiring. So, maximizing for salary first is almost always the right approach.

If you're not getting the salary you want, though—and even if you are—you can negotiate on other parts of your employment package. For example, imagine that you get an offer for $55,000 per year. You wanted $60,000 per year but the $55,000 is above your minimum and they're holding firm at $55,000. You could counter by letting them know that you wanted $60,000 per year, but would be willing to accept their offer if they'd pay up to $2,000 per year in conference admission and travel expenses and give you 2 more paid days off per year.

You could also negotiate adding a Health Savings Account to your health benefits and funding it $200 per month. Or you could ask for a dental or vision plan in addition to your health insurance.

You could push for a bigger desk area, better desk location, gym membership, or some other perks as well.

Just make sure that you've gotten as far as you can with salary negotiations first, then push for other things.

10.5 Walking Away

If the company cannot give you an offer you're happy with, walk away. Developers today have so many opportunities that unless your expectations are wildly out of whack with reality, you should be able to find another company that will give you the offer you are looking for.

Chapter 11: Conclusion

Hopefully by now you understand why doing the traditional job search doesn't work.

Let me quickly recap the steps you're going to take to jumpstart your ability to find your dream developer job.

11.1 Update Your Resume

When you get noticed by a company or find a company you want to work for, it's easier to update an already up-to-date resume with details you find in your research than it is to create a new one from scratch. It also gives you something to hand off or email to someone on short notice.

11.2 Find and Join a Local Users' Group

Find a local group of developers that you can get involved with. Ask people where they work and what they like about their employer. Help organize events, speak, or find other ways to contribute so people will want to have you around. Remind people that you're looking for a job.

11.3 Start a Side Project

Nothing demonstrates your ability to deliver than having already delivered. Don't miss out on an opportunity to give yourself something to talk about and code for others to review. Have the code reviewed by senior people frequently and take the opportunity to learn.

11.4 Figure Out What You Want

Find out the top 3 things that you need in that job to make you happy. Work through the guide in Chapter 3 to figure out what those things are and then keep them in mind while you research the companies you find.

11.5 Research Companies You're Applying To

As companies come across your radar, look into them to see what they are doing that indicate to you that they're the align with the Top 3 that you outlined when designing your dream job. Also spend time figuring out what they're looking for and how they determine that candidates match up.

11.6 Stand Out

Put yourself in a position to get noticed by people who work for the company you're targeting or companies like it. Once you've got their attention, build a relationship that will make them want to go advocate for you with their boss.

11.7 Send a Customized Resume and Cover Letter to the Company You're Applying To

Once you know what a company is looking for and how they decide that you line up with that description, update your resume to reflect those qualities. Explain in your cover letter how you work toward those ideals. Send that in through an employee that you met or found during your research.

11.8 Practice for Interviews

Make sure that you spend time practicing the tools, technologies, and interview strategies that will allow you to put your best foot forward. Be relaxed. Be honest. Do your best. You've got this!

11.9 Negotiate Your Salary

Make at least one counter offer. Don't tell them what you want, but let them offer and then counteroffer to get closer to your ideal setup.

11.10 You Can Do This

The question isn't whether you're worthy, it's whether you can do the work.

In almost everything in life, people become qualified for the work they do after doing it for a period of time. Your job in looking for a job is to demonstrate that you're the type of person who can deliver results, and then to knock it out of the park once you're in the door.

www.ingramcontent.com/pod-product-compliance
Lightning Source LLC
Chambersburg PA
CBHW070616220526
45466CB00001B/12